WordPress MU 2.8
Beginner's Guide

Build your own blog network with unlimited users and blogs,
forums, photo galleries, and more!

Lesley A. Harrison

BIRMINGHAM - MUMBAI

WordPress MU 2.8
Beginner's Guide

First published: October 2009

Production Reference: 1211009

Published by Packt Publishing Ltd.
32 Lincoln Road
Olton
Birmingham, B27 6PA, UK.

ISBN 978-1-847196-54-5

www.packtpub.com

Cover Image by Vinayak Chittar (vinayak.chittar@gmail.com)

Credits

Author
Lesley A. Harrison

Reviewers
Joseph Arellano
Lee Jordon

Acquisition Editor
David Barnes

Development Editor
Amey Kanse

Technical Editor
Gaurav Datar

Copy Editor
Sanchari Mukherjee

Indexer
Hemangini Bari

Editorial Team Leader
Gagandeep Singh

Project Team Leader
Priya Mukherji

Project Coordinator
Zainab Bagasrawala

Proofreader
Jade Schuler

Production Coordinator
Shantanu Zagade

Cover Work
Shantanu Zagade

About the Author

Lesley Harrison has more than ten years of experience working in the world of IT. She has served as a web developer for various local organizations, a systems administrator for a multinational IT outsourcing company, and later a database administrator for a British utility company. Today, Lesley runs her own video gaming site, Myth-Games.com, and works as a freelance web developer. She works with clients all over the world to develop Joomla! and WordPress/WordPress MU web sites.

Lesley has enjoyed seeing the Internet develop from the days of newsgroups and static HTML pages, to the vast and interactive World Wide Web of today.

She worked as a reviewer on Daniel Chapman's *Joomla 1.5 Customization* book, which was published by Packt Publishing in August 2009.

I would like to thank my husband Mark for his patience while I was writing this book instead of leveling one of my many characters. I would also like to thank Blaenk Denum for his help with the reCAPTCHA plugin, and the Packt Publishing team for their patience and guidance over the past year.

About the Reviewers

Lee Jordon is an avid user of WordPress, Blogger, Twitter, and other useful web applications. She designs interactive customer service portals, enterprise-level web sites, other web-based applications, and writes web content and user guides. Her toolbox includes HTML, PHP, JavaScript, Java Servlets, MySQL, Flash, Dreamweaver, and Photoshop. She applies over 10 years of experience of designing and writing for the Web to develop interactive, user friendly web sites and writing technical guides to popular web technologies. She is the author of two books with Packt Publishing: *Blogger: Beyond the Basics* and *Project Management with dotProject*.

Joseph Arellano holds a B.A. in Communication Arts from the University of the Pacific and a J.D. (law degree) from the University of Southern California. He lives in Northern California and maintains the Joseph's Reviews book review blogsite (`http://josephsreviews.wordpress.com/`).

Table of Contents

Preface

In today's digital world, it seems that everyone has a web presence—be that a profile on a social networking site such as Facebook, a blog hosted by Blogger or WordPress.com, or their own web site.

General networking and blogging sites are useful for keeping in touch with old friends, but their search tools are less effective if you are trying to find people with similar interests to your own or who work in the same industry.

The multiuser version of WordPress, called WordPress MU, is an ideal solution to this problem. WordPress MU, paired with forum software such as bbPress and the BuddyPress suite of social networking tools, allows you to start your own blog network with social networking features such as friends lists, status updates, and groups. Using these tools, you could start a social network and blogging site for a local social group, a fan club, or your company.

Throughout this book, we will build a blog network called SlayerCafe. This blog network is aimed at Vampire Slayers and their Watchers, as well as other people who are interested in joining the fight against demons of the night. The Slayers and Watchers will be able to share information, swap tips, update each other on their activities, share videos, and discuss demonic goings-on in the site's forums. The Slayers feel they need such a site because they found that public social networking sites such as Facebook weren't suitable for discussing vampires and werewolves. Their serious conversations were invaded by fans of *Vampire: The Masquerade* and *Twilight*, which made it too difficult to separate the real vampires from the fictional ones.

This book will explain how to set up WordPress MU and how to seamlessly integrate WordPress MU with bbPress and BuddyPress. You will also learn how to promote your blog network and attract new users, as well as how to keep your site safe, secure, and free from spam.

Running a successful blog network requires a good web server; however, it does not have to be expensive to get started. You will learn about the different hosting options available to you, along with the ways to optimize WordPress MU so that the server load is reduced as much as possible.

If your site is a business venture, then you will be interested in learning how to make money by charging for premium memberships, selling site-related merchandise, or by using advertising. All those options will be discussed.

What this book covers

Chapter 1—Introducing WordPress MU will introduce WordPress MU, bbPress, and BuddyPress and explain the hosting requirements of those sites. You will learn about shared hosting, Virtual Private Servers (known as VPSes), and dedicated servers, and you will get an overview of the benefits and downsides of each of those hosting options. Finally, you will learn how to plan the development of your site so that it has all of the features that you want to offer to your prospective users.

Chapter 2—Installing WordPress MU will discuss setting up a local copy of your site for testing purposes and installing WordPress MU on your web server in subdomain configuration so that users can have WordPress.com style "myusername.theblogsite.com" blog addresses.

Chapter 3—Customizing the Appearance of Your Site will cover installing and customizing themes and how to offer a range of theme choices to your users. You will also be introduced to some plug-ins that offer community features so that your blog looks like it is a part of a network, rather than a standalone blog.

Chapter 4—Letting Users Manage Their Blogs will cover more about the multiuser aspects of WordPress MU and setting up some features that allow users to manage their blogs, including allowing them to add and remove plugins and widgets, change their themes, and even have their own domain name point to their blog.

Chapter 5—Protecting Your Site will explore some security options that will make life harder for spammers and hackers, keeping the site clean, safe, and stable for your users. You will learn how to reduce spam, block known bad visitors, and automate backups, so that if the worst happens, you can restore a backup of your site quickly and easily.

Chapter 6—Increasing Traffic to Your Blog Network discusses some simple promotion techniques that will make it easy for you and your site's users to bring in visitors to their blogs. You will learn how to offer RSS feeds that interested visitors can subscribe to, and how to "converse" with other bloggers via trackbacks. You will also learn how to use pings to tell blog directories that your blog has been updated and how to promote your blog on Twitter.

Chapter 7—Sticky Features for your Blog Network tells what is meant by a "sticky" site and how to make your visitors feel like they are part of the community, encouraging them to return to the site and promote your site to their friends.

Chapter 8—Adding Forums with bbPress introduces the bbPress forum software. You will learn how to install it and how to integrate it seamlessly with WordPress MU. Not only will the two parts of the site look like they fit together, but they will behave like they are part of the same site, too. Your users will need to register for an account once and, when they log in to the site, they will have access to both the blog network and the forums.

Chapter 9—Social Networking with BuddyPress will help us add some social features to our site. BuddyPress offers several features, including friends lists, groups, and The Wire (a feature similar to Facebook's Wall). Along with setting up and optimizing BuddyPress, you will learn how to allow your users to log in to your site with Facebook Connect and how to integrate BuddyPress with Twitter—the popular "microblogging" service.

Chapter 10—Monetizing Your Site will show how to monetize your site. We will explore several different options, including advertising, revenue sharing, donations, and subscriptions. Which model (or models) you choose will depend on the kind of community you are running. You will learn about several different revenue models so that you can find the one that suits your site best.

Chapter 11—Site Optimization will explain some ways to reduce the load generated by your visitors, enabling your existing server to handle a greater amount of traffic. You will also learn about some cheaper ways to increase your server's capacity.

Chapter 12—Troubleshooting and Maintaining your Site will give an overview of how to maintain your site and how to troubleshoot common issues with upgrades and plugins. You will see some common error messages and learn what they are likely to mean and how to fix them.

Who this book is for

If you wish to manage multiple blogs and build a blog network, then this book is for you. You are not expected to be experienced with PHP coding. Some knowledge of HTML and some experience with the blogging and social networking world will be helpful, but not essential.

Conventions

In this book, you will find a number of styles of text that distinguish between different kinds of information. Here are some examples of these styles, and an explanation of their meaning.

Code words in text are shown as follows: "Open your theme's `index.php` file—in our case we are editing the Blue Zinfandel theme."

A block of code will be set as follows:

```php
<?php
    $email = $authordata->user_email;
    $hash = md5($email);
    $uri = 'http://www.gravatar.com/avatar/' . $hash . '?d=identicon&r
=any&size=80';
    $headers = wp_get_http_headers($uri);
```

Any command-line input or output is written as follows:

```
Mysqldump –add-drop-table –h localhost –u username –p databasename | gzip
-c > backup_wpmu.sql.gzip
```

New terms and **important words** are shown in bold. Words that you see on the screen, in menus or dialog boxes for example, appear in our text like this: " You can add new fields using the **Generate Tag** dropdown ".

 Warnings or important notes appear in a box like this.

 Tips and tricks appear like this.

Reader feedback

Feedback from our readers is always welcome. Let us know what you think about this book—what you liked or may have disliked. Reader feedback is important for us to develop titles that you really get the most out of.

To send us general feedback, simply drop an email to feedback@packtpub.com, and mention the book title in the subject of your message.

If there is a book that you need and would like to see us publish, please send us a note in the **SUGGEST A TITLE** form on www.packtpub.com or email suggest@packtpub.com.

If there is a topic that you have expertise in and you are interested in either writing or contributing to a book, see our author guide on www.packtpub.com/authors.

Customer support

Now that you are the proud owner of a Packt book, we have a number of things to help you to get the most from your purchase.

Downloading the example code for the book

Visit http://www.packtpub.com/files/code/6545_Code.zip to directly download the example code.

The downloadable files contain instructions on how to use them.

Errata

Although we have taken every care to ensure the accuracy of our contents, mistakes do happen. If you find a mistake in one of our books—maybe a mistake in text or code—we would be grateful if you would report this to us. By doing so, you can save other readers from frustration, and help us to improve subsequent versions of this book. If you find any errata, please report them by visiting http://www.packtpub.com/support, selecting your book, clicking on the **let us know** link, and entering the details of your errata. Once your errata are verified, your submission will be accepted and the errata added to any list of existing errata. Any existing errata can be viewed by selecting your title from http://www.packtpub.com/support.

Piracy

Piracy of copyright material on the Internet is an ongoing problem across all media. At Packt, we take the protection of our copyright and licenses very seriously. If you come across any illegal copies of our works in any form on the Internet, please provide us with the location address or website name immediately so that we can pursue a remedy.

Please contact us at copyright@packtpub.com with a link to the suspected pirated material.

We appreciate your help in protecting our authors, and our ability to bring you valuable content.

Questions

You can contact us at questions@packtpub.com if you are having a problem with any aspect of the book, and we will do our best to address it.

1
Introducing WordPress MU

It seems as if everyone has a blog these days—whether it's a work-related one, a platform for launching a writing career, or just somewhere to upload random musings and holiday snaps. Many people maintain several different blogs, each one focused on a different subject. If you run a web site, offering your members the ability to run a blog is a great way to encourage repeat visitors and build a sense of community. Throughout this book, we will be working on building a web site called The SlayerCafe. This web site will use WordPress MU to offer its members the chance to create their own blogs. It will also use bbPress-powered forums and BuddyPress for social networking features.

The SlayerCafe is aimed at Slayers, their Watchers, and people (including good-aligned Werewolves, Techno Mages, and Wiccans) who would like to join in the fight against vampires. The blog network will allow the site's users to share advice and information in the form of blog posts, videos, and comments. The social side of the site will allow Slayers and Watchers to create special interest groups, engage in discussions in forums, and update their status feeds so that their fellow community members know what's going on at all times. The SlayerCafe will make use of Facebook Connect and tie in to the Twitter micro-blogging service, too.

A basic membership to SlayerCafe will be free, and there will be some advertisements on the site to support this, but there will also be premium memberships with special features available only to paying members.

In this chapter you will learn about:

- WordPress MU—which allows you to offer blogs to your users
- BuddyPress—which helps you turn your WordPress MU site into a social network
- bbPress—which allows you to run forums from your WordPress MU site
- The tools you need to get the above scripts up and running

So let's get started...

What is WordPress MU

You may already be familiar with WordPress, either through the free blog site WordPress.com or the blog script that you can download from WordPress.org. WordPress MU allows you to run your own site in the vein of WordPress.com. It is ideal for people who want to run multiple blogs or who want to offer blog hosting services to their users.

You may be wondering why you would use WordPress MU to run several blogs on the same domain, instead of just installing a new blog each time. Well, with WordPress MU, all the blogs are stored in the same database (without your worrying about coming up with unique table prefixes), and all of the blogs run off one install. This means you only have to update one install when new versions are released and, when it comes to editing source code or uploading plugins, you only have to do those jobs once.

Most WordPress plugins, widgets, and themes are compatible with WordPress MU, so you have a huge range of designs and features available to you, as well as the option of coding your own designs and features if you are a skilled programmer or designer.

The developers of WordPress are planning to merge the WordPress and WordPress MU projects at some point in the future. Therefore, learning how to use the multisite features of WordPress MU now will help you stand in good stead for the future when users of the single-site version are looking for designers to help them convert their site to a multiblog platform. For more information about the project and the plans to merge it with the single-site version of WordPress, check the official WordPress MU site at http://mu.wordpress.org, along with http://ocaoimh.ie/—the blog of Donncha, one of the WordPress developers .

WordPress MU can be downloaded from http://mu.wordpress.org/download/.

The WordPress MU community is not as large as the WordPress community; however, it is still very active and there are lots of places you can turn to for assistance with your site. The official help channels are:

- The WordPress MU forums (`http://mu.wordpress.org/forums/`).
- The WordPress MU IRC Channel on Freenode. Connection instructions can be found at `http://codex.wordpress.org/WPMU_IRC_Channel`.
- The bug tracker, available at `http://trac.mu.wordpress.org/`.
- The MU page of the WordPress Codex: `http://codex.wordpress.org/index.php?title=Category:WPMU`.

WordPress MU's features include:

- Unlimited blogs
- Unlimited authors on each blog
- Each user can have more than one blog (or none at all!)
- Users can have different roles on different blogs
- Blogs can have different plugins and different themes
- Blogs can be hosted on subdomains (`myblog.mysite.com`) or in subdirectories (`mysite.com/myblog`)

Users will be able to register at your site and request a blog, which will be created automatically. The blog admin panel looks a lot like the standard WordPress blog admin panel (as you can see in the below screenshot), so it will be familiar to many of your users.

WordPress Moo?

WordPress MU is sometimes seen written as WordPress- μ (using the Greek letter "Mu".) In fact, the use of that symbol was originally the preference of the developers. If the Greek symbol is used, then the μ is pronounced as "Mew". Over time, writing the name as "WordPress MU" has become the popular preference, and the popular pronunciation of the name is "WordPress Em Yew". Some people prefer to say "Moo" and this is also considered to be a valid pronunciation.

Making your own social blog network

A blog network is all well and good, but how will your users find each other? How will they talk to each other? Building a sense of community is important if you want your site to succeed. Even corporate blog networks can benefit from community-like features. For example, your users could set up groups for teams or departments to share information with each other and have private discussions.

There are two very useful plugins that make it easy to add social features to WordPress MU. One is BuddyPress that adds Facebook-like features to WordPress MU. The other is bbPress that you can use to integrate forums with your blog. We will discuss bbPress in Chapter 8 and BuddyPress in Chapter 9.

What is BuddyPress

BuddyPress is a suite of plugins for WordPress MU. These plugins allow you to add social networking features to your site, including friends lists, private messages, photo galleries, status feeds, and more.

The complete suite of BuddyPress plugins includes:

- **Extended Profiles**: Add extra information to your users' profiles.

- **Private Messaging**: Make it easy for members to contact their friends on-site.

- **Friends Lists**: Allow your users to maintain a list of their on-site friends, and see who others have added as friends.

- **Groups**: Allow users to create and join groups on any topic they choose. Groups have their own "wires", forums and news pages.

- **The Wire**: Site users can visit a member's wire and post messages to it. This is similar to a Facebook Wall.

- **Activity Streams**: Members can post updates to their activity stream. This is similar to a Twitter stream or Facebook Status Update.

BuddyPress sits on top of WordPress MU and is installed much like a normal plugin. You don't have to install all the features. If you want only Friends Lists and Activity Streams, you can choose to use just those plugins, or you could simply install everything. The choice is yours.

You can find out more about BuddyPress at `http://buddypress.org/`.

What is bbPress

bbPress is a forum plugin for WordPress and WordPress MU sites. It was made by the developers of WordPress and is easy to integrate with an existing WordPress or WordPress MU blog.

Some people prefer to use other standalone forum scripts such as VBulletin, phpBB, or SMF with WordPress MU and use a "bridge" to tie together the login details from the two databases. This can work well and is certainly a good option if you have a reason for wanting to use a standalone forum. (Perhaps you have already purchased a license for VBulletin, or you have a heavily modified phpBB install with a large user base, and don't want to confuse your users by making a change.)

However, if you are building a brand new site, then the advantages of bbPress are huge.

- bbPress has been developed from the ground up to work with WordPress and WordPress MU.
- It can easily be modified to share the theme of your WordPress site.
- It has "pretty permalinks", just like WordPress.
- It is stable and fast.
- The ties to WordPress mean that when new versions of bbPress or WordPress are released, any integration issues will be fixed promptly.
- There are lots of plugins available to add new features to your forum.

You can find out more about bbPress at `http://bbpress.org/`.

Making and hosting my site

You will need a very good hosting package to run a busy social networking and blogging site. In most cases, a shared hosting package will not be able to handle the load, even if, on paper, the package meets the requirements listed on the WordPress MU site.

You can run small WordPress MU sites on a shared host. In fact, if you know that your site will have only a small number of users (for example, if your site is aimed at members of a club or society or is used by your company's employees), then shared hosting may be all that you need.

If you're unsure how popular your site will be, look for a host that offers easy upgrades from shared hosting to a VPS or dedicated hosting so that you can upgrade if you need to. If you are creating a site for use by members of the public, don't rush out to buy a server and pay a fortune on collocation straightaway. Start small and upgrade when you need to.

Choose your host carefully

A shared hosting account may be sufficient to install and test your web site, but it is likely that you will quickly reach the limits of a shared host once your site opens to the public. WordPress MU uses more server resources than a standalone WordPress blog, and you should make sure that your host will be able to cope with the demand. For a small or medium sized community, a low-end VPS account will probably be the best choice. The good news is that VPS accounts are only slightly more expensive than a good shared hosting account and, for your money, you will get a server that can grow with you as your traffic increases.

Choosing between VPS, dedicated, and grid hosting

The range of hosting options out there can be quite intimidating, especially if you aren't used to managing your own sites. The kind of hosting you choose will depend on the amount of traffic your site gets, your budget, and the features you need access to.

VPS

A **VPS** is a **Virtual Private Server**. This is the next step up from standard shared hosting. With a VPS, you have a shell account and total control over your server. You can install whatever you want and configure it the way you want. VPSes aren't actually real physical boxes; they are virtual machines, and your VPS is likely to be running on the same computer as several other VPSes.

The good thing about VPSes is that they are inexpensive, and you have almost total control over the configuration of the machine. However, VPS packages tend to be less powerful than dedicated hosting packages, so you may find that if your site takes off, you outgrow your VPS very quickly.

If you aren't already familiar with running a server, then you may want to consider buying a "Managed VPS" package. These are more expensive than standard packages, but your hosting company will look after the technical side of things, including applying security patches when they are released and managing the configuration of the server.

Dedicated servers

Dedicated servers are much more expensive than VPSes. But instead of just getting a small virtual machine and limited bandwidth and storage space, you get a real, physical server. If you need the freedom to do whatever you want and expect to have very high traffic, then leasing a dedicated server is a good option. You could also consider buying a server and then using a collocation agreement.

Grid hosting

Grid hosting is a relatively new form of hosting. Instead of all your scripts and data being handled in one central place, it is handled "in the cloud". Cloud-based hosting solutions can be economical if you are expecting small amounts of traffic most of the time but want to make sure that a sudden traffic spike won't bring your server to its knees. Usually, you pay for only the amount of bandwidth/processor cycles you use, and the servers respond elastically to your needs.

The downside of grid hosting is that many grid hosts don't support wildcard subdomains, and you can't tweak your server's configuration the way you can with a dedicated server. Also, if you're running under high load all the time, your bills could work out to be more expensive than with a dedicated server.

For most people, a dedicated server or a VPS is the best option. You could always farm out specific parts of your site to the cloud. We will discuss how to do this later in the book.

Server requirements for WordPress MU

You can run WordPress MU on most web servers. The developers recommend Apache or LiteSpeed, but it is possible to run WordPress MU on other servers such as Lighttpd or Nginx, although alternative web servers may require some tweaks that are beyond the scope of this book. The main requirements are:

- PHP version 4.3 or newer
- MySQL version 4.1.2 or newer
- Apache `mod_rewrite` (or similar URL rewriting support if you are using an alternative server type)

If you want to take advantage of the subdomains feature of WordPress MU, then you will need access to the WHM control panel (or have some other way of setting up wildcard subdomains). If you are using a VPS or dedicated server, you can set up the subdomains yourself using Bind 9. If you're on a shared host, you may need to contact support to get them to set up wildcard subdomains for you.

Other things to check with your host:

- The PHP memory limit: You should ensure it can be increased to at least 32MB (preferably 64MB)
- `Register_globals` should be turned off in `php.ini`.

Recommended WordPress MU hosts

If you don't have a web host yet or have found that your existing web host can't quite handle WordPress MU, you can find recommendations for a good host on the WordPress MU forums.

Here are some suggestions to get you started:

- `http://www.dreamhost.com`: It offers shared hosting. It is inexpensive and good if you expect to host only a small number of blogs.
- `http://www.futurehost.biz`: More expensive, but better support. Offers a good range of package choices for busier blog networks.

I use a UK-based web hosting company called 34SP (`http://www.34sp.com`). Their prices are in GBP and their packages aren't quite as generous on data transfer/storage as some of the deals offered by other hosts, but I have been with them for almost four years and have found their servers to be rock-solid stable and their tech support team is very knowledgeable and quick to respond.

Building our example site: The SlayerCafe

Throughout this book we will be building a niche blog network—for Vampire Slayers. The site, called SlayerCafe, will offer a safe environment for Vampire Slayers, Watchers, and other people who are interested in fighting against vampires and demons.

SlayerCafe will provide its members with their own blog (which can be set to private if they wish), and it will also allow them to form special interest groups, build friends lists of local Slayers, and share information with each other.

To ensure that the Watchers that run the site don't have too much of their time eaten up by boring admin tasks (they still have to research vampires and guide their Slayers, after all!), we will set up some anti-spam measures and assign some senior Slayers with moderator roles so that they can take care of the basic admin tasks on the site.

We will also put in place some security measures to ensure that our site isn't taken down by angry vampire hackers.

Running a site can be expensive. If SlayerCafe becomes popular with the Slayers, then they will use up a lot of bandwidth posting photographs and videos of their exploits!

To combat this bandwidth bill, we will offer premium membership features, such as the ability to customize your theme, extra storage space, and custom ranks on the forums, and we will run a SlayerCafe store where members can purchase t-shirts and other items.

Planning your site

It's easy to get carried away when you are trying to plan your WordPress MU site. There are thousands of plugins and widgets available and, if you install all the ones that sound cool, you'll end up with a site that is very cluttered and difficult to use.

When planning your site, think about what it is you want the site to do. The chances are, you want most (if not all) of the features offered by the basic bbPress and BuddyPress. You will also want some of the plugins that make life easier for the site admin (anti-spam measures, plugin management, and so on), but when you're thinking about the frontend that your users see, try to keep it as clean as possible.

Consider the following:

+ **Your target audience**: You may think that a Twitter widget is cool, but if your site is aimed at teenagers, do some research to see what social networks they prefer. You may find a Twitter widget wouldn't be wanted, while other networks would go down well.

+ **The purpose of the site**: The ability to share PowerPoint presentations is a must-have feature for a work-related site, but on a more social site, users may prefer being able to share videos instead.

+ **Expected browsers and screen sizes**: If you're creating a site for your company, you know what browser is installed and what screen size most people use. If your site is aimed at people who play video games, you can reasonably expect they will have large screens and run a modern browser. If it's aimed at a niche interest group that isn't something to do with technology, then it's worth catering to older browsers and smaller screen resolutions and picking a theme that will look good on as many different setups as possible.

The beauty of WordPress MU is that it is easy to add and remove features, and your site can grow over time. Rather than overwhelming your visitors, start small by offering them the features they really need. As your member base grows, listen to their feedback and gradually add the features they want. This should ensure that everything on your site is practical and that you don't end up with a "monster site" with lots of features that hardly anyone uses and are nothing more than an inconvenience when they break.

Summary

This chapter introduced WordPress MU, BuddyPress, and bbPress, and talked about choosing a host for your site, as well as looking ahead to what we will cover in the rest of the book.

In this chapter we learned about WordPress MU and how it differs from the single-user version of WordPress. We also learned about BuddyPress and bbPress—what they are used for, what each part of the script does, and why you would want to use them. We learned about the social features of BuddyPress and the benefits of using bbPress instead of a piece of standalone forum software.

We also learned about the web hosting requirements of WordPress MU. We talked about the different kinds of hosting available, and the kinds of site that would suit each hosting option.

We also discussed how to plan your site and choose which features you want to add to your blog network. We talked about the example site, SlayerCafe, that we will be building throughout the course of this book.

Now that we know what we will be using to build our site, it's time to start building it. In Chapter 2, we will install WordPress MU.

2
Installing WordPress MU

Now that we know what WordPress MU can do and the kind of site that we would like to have, it's time to start putting a site together.

In this chapter we will:

- ◆ Set up a local version of WordPress MU
- ◆ Set up a live version on our chosen hosting account
- ◆ Learn how to give our users attractive subdomain addresses for their blogs

Let's get started!

Tools you will need

If you have already set up your own WordPress blog, right from the beginning you will probably have the tools you need to get started with WordPress MU. All you need is a plain text editor and an FTP client. As your experience grows, you may find that you want to add to your arsenal some other tools such as browser plugins that will help you tweak and debug your site from within your browser.

Text editors

For Windows users, I recommend one of the following text editors:

- ◆ Notepad++ (http://notepad-plus.sourceforge.net)
- ◆ Crimson Editor (http://www.crimsoneditor.com/)

Both of these are free applications. (Notepad++ is open source.)

For Mac users I recommend Aptana (`http://aptana.com/`). Linux users can try JEdit (`http://www.jedit.org`) or see if their favorite text editor has syntax highlighting capabilities.

FTP clients and other tools

For an FTP client, I recommend FileZilla (`http://filezilla-project.org/`). This FTP client is free and has versions available for Windows, Mac, and Linux. Another option for Windows users is Core FTP LE (`http://www.coreftp.com/`).

If you use the Firefox web browser (`http://www.getfirefox.com`), you may find the following browser plugins useful:

- Firebug: For editing and debugging HTML and CSS in your browser, available at `https://addons.mozilla.org/en-US/firefox/addon/1843`
- YSlow: For determining why a page is taking long to load, available at `https://addons.mozilla.org/en-US/firefox/addon/5369`
- ColorZilla: A useful color picker for your browser, available at `https://addons.mozilla.org/en-US/firefox/addon/271`

Setting up a local web server

Let's start by setting up a local web server. We will use this to make a local installation of WordPress MU, which will serve as a private testing ground.

It is a good idea to have a local copy of your site. It lets you test things quickly and easily and ensures that should any of your edits go wrong, nobody else will see. Editing your site while it is live can annoy your visitors, especially if the edits don't work as expected on the first attempt. Testing on a private server minimizes the risk of any unnecessary downtime. If you don't want to run a test server, skip to the *Time for action – working with cPanel* section.

Time for action – getting your server set up

There are lots of free web server packages available. I recommend WAMP (`http://www.wampserver.com/en/`) for Windows and MAMP (`http://www.mamp.info/`) for Mac users. Both of these packages provide Apache, MySQL, and PHP—the **AMP** part of the acronyms WAMP and MAMP. The W stands for Windows and M for Mac. If you're on Linux, then there should be a LAMP package available for your distribution. One option is XAMPP (the final P stands for Perl), which you should be able to install through your distribution's package manager. XAMPP is also available for other platforms. This book assumes you are using Windows, so the following instructions are for the WAMP package:

1. Download the appropriate server package for your operating system.

2. Run the installer. In most cases accepting the default settings is fine.

3. Set your default browser. The installer defaults to Internet Explorer.

4. Click the WAMPServer icon in the system tray and navigate to **Apache | Apache Modules**. Scroll through the list until you see rewrite module and click it to enable it.

5. Select WAMPServer in the system tray and go to **Apache | Service | Test Port 80**.

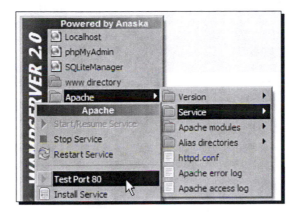

6. A window will appear telling you if anything else is using Port 80. The two most common issues I have seen are existing IIS servers and Skype. Close any applications that the server warns you about.

7. Activate the server using the WAMPServer icon in the system tray by clicking **Start All Services** and then **Put Online**.

8. Launch your browser and go to `http://localhost/`. You should see something like the following:

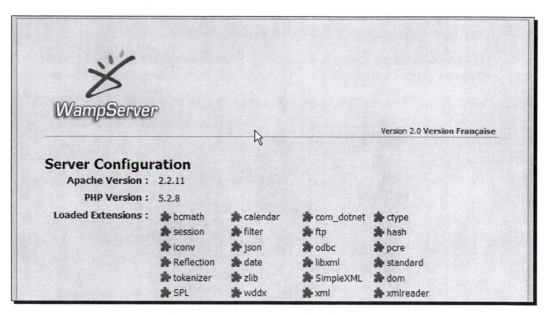

What just happened?

Congratulations! You now have a web server running on your local machine. The server name stands for Windows (or Linux / Mac), Apache (the web server), MySQL (the database server), and PHP (the scripting language that WordPress MU uses). The rewrite module is also known as `mod_rewrite`. We had to enable this because WordPress MU uses it to create easy-to-read URLs for your users' blogs.

Now, let's get our local web server ready for action.

Databases with MySQL

WordPress MU needs a database to store blog posts, user information, and so on. We will be using MySQL to provide this database. The default installation of WAMPServer does not set a password for the root MySQL user. This is convenient, but could be dangerous, depending on how your computer is set up. If you are running some firewall software or using a router, you can leave the root password unset. However, if you will be allowing people outside your network to connect to your local server, then you should set the root password. You can find out how to do this by reading the phpMyAdmin documentation at `http://www.phpmyadmin.net/home_page/docs.php`.

Preparing for WordPress MU—creating a database

Now that our MySQL server is a little more secure, let's get back to WordPress MU. When you install WordPress MU, it will ask you for connection details for a database. We will need to create this database and set up a user for it.

Time for action – creating a database for WordPress MU

1. Open phpMyAdmin in your browser.

2. Enter a simple but clear name for the database—I've chosen **slayerblogs**. Now click **Create**.

MySQL localhost

Create new database ⑦

| slayerblogs | Collation ▼ |

Create

Naming your database

Some shared web hosts prepend your username to all database names. For example, if your username is "lhar1" and you chose "slayerblogs" as the database name, it would come out as "lhar1_slayerblogs". If you want to have identical setups on both the live and local servers, double-check the naming conventions of your web host before creating your local database.

3. Now you'll need to create a user, which WordPress MU will use to access the database. To do this, click on the Home icon located on the lefthand side of the page.

4. Select the **Privileges** tab and click **add new user**.

5. Enter the username and password into the relevant field.

6. Select **Localhost** for the **host** field. Leave the other fields as default.

7. Don't set any privileges yet. Just scroll down and click **Go**.

8. Scroll down to **Database Specific Privileges** and select your database. Then click **Go**.

9. In the **Global Privileges** section, click **Check All**, and then click **Go**. You should see a confirmation screen like the following:

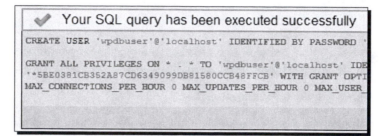

What just happened?

We have set up a database for WordPress MU to store the content, along with a user that WordPress MU can use to connect to this database. Remember these details, as we will need them when we start the installation of the site.

Time for action – subdomains for WordPress MU

WordPress MU doesn't like running under `http://localhost/`. Instead of using a simple hostname, it needs a two-part Fully Qualified Domain Name. We will need to edit our Windows `Hosts` file so that we can use `http://localhost.localdomain/` as a valid address for our local server.

1. Using your favorite text editor, open your `hosts` file. On most of the versions of Windows you will find this file at `C:\windows\system32\drivers\etc`. The `hosts` file is simply called `hosts` with no extension, so you may not be able to see it in the **File | Open** dialog of your text editor. Instead, navigate to the correct folder, right-click on the file, and select **Open**.

2. Leave any existing text alone. Add the following lines to the bottom of the file:

```
127.0.0.1      localhost.localdomain
127.0.0.1      slayercafe.localhost.localdomain
```

3. Save the file and browse to `http://localhost.localdomain` in your web browser. You should see your WAMPServer welcome page. Your antivirus software may warn you that your `hosts` file has been edited. You can safely ignore this message.

What just happened?

The `hosts` file is used by Windows to determine the location of network addresses. We have set it up so that our computer knows that the addresses `localhost.localdomain` and `slayer.localhost.localdomain` belong to our computer.

The `localhost.localdomain` address is used as the home page for WordPress MU on our local machine. The slayer address will be used by our test user. WordPress MU relies on the Apache module called `mod_rewrite` to interpret requests for specific URLs and to rewrite the request into something WordPress MU understands. For example, on our live server, a request to `buffy.slayercafe.com` will be interpreted as a request for the blog owned by the user "buffy". If there is no such user, WordPress will display a page saying that the blog does not exist and invite the visitor to sign up and create a blog.

Pop quiz – your local server

Congratulations! You're now running your own server.

The first thing I'd suggest you to do is make a backup, while everything is working nicely! While you're doing that, let's test your server knowledge.

1. The MySQL root user is:

    a) Just the default login account, and not very important.

    b) The user you should use for all database actions.

    c) An account that has access to all databases and should be protected by a good password.

    d) The user account made for your gardener.

Answer: C

Have a go hero – getting more from Apache

If your WordPress MU site is going to be a group endeavor, why not look into using a service such as `http://www.dyndns.com/` to make it easy for your friends and colleagues to access it from the outside.

If you want to tinker more with the server, try setting up some custom error pages. WordPress MU handles some errors for you (for example, Error 404), but many others are handled by Apache. Open the `httpd.conf` file and search for `ErrorDocument` to see some examples. Don't change anything except the `ErrorDocument` lines.

Preparing your live server

Your test server is ready for WordPress MU now, but we still need to get the live server working. For the purposes of this chapter, I will assume that your web host uses cPanel. If they use Plesk or some other form of control panel, check your host's support pages for assistance.

Time for action – working with cPanel

Just follow the steps mentioned next to configure your live server:

1. Log in to your site's cPanel. The address for this will most likely be included in the email your host sent you when you created an account.

2. Click on the MySQL Databases icon—this is usually the picture of a dolphin.

3. Enter the name of the database you want to use for WordPress MU and click **create database**.

4. Create a new user and enter a secure password. Make a note of the password you enter, as you will need it later.

5. Scroll down to the **Add Users To Your Database** section and select your new user and database. Leave the **All** box checked and click **Add User to Database**.

What just happened?

Good news! That was the last preparatory step before we can get on with installing WordPress MU. cPanel makes it easy to set up users and databases. WordPress MU will need the login details that we just created so that it can connect to our MySQL server and store setup information, along with the information relating to blogs that users will create on our blog network.

User blogs with subdomains

We've already decided that we'd like to give our users attractive blog addresses. To accomplish this, we need to enable wildcard subdomains. These make sure that every time a new user creates a blog, their `myblog.slayercafe.com` address will work right away.

Time for action – subdomains under WHM

1. Log in to your WHM control panel. This is a feature of most good cPanel hosts and is usually found on port 2087; so, in our case that would be `http://slayercafe.com:2087`. (Your host may use a different port, in which case you may need to consult your host's support pages.)

2. Click on **DNS Functions**. Then click on **Edit DNS Zone** when the next screen appears.

3. Select the domain name of your WordPress MU site and select **Edit**. Scroll down to the section that says **Add New Entries Below this Line** and create a new *A record* with the value * . The 'IP or Hostname' box should contain the IP address of the site:

4. Click **Save** and then reopen the **Edit Zone** page to make sure the change was saved correctly. If the records are still there, great! It will take a while for the change to actually affect the site, but you can be confident it has worked.

Finding your site's IP

If you aren't sure what the IP address of your site is, you can find it either by looking at the other records listed in the zone (the *A record* for the site's domain name itself will contain the IP of the site) or by opening a command prompt and typing `mydomain.com`. The IP address is the four sets of numbers after **Reply from** when the command runs.

What just happened?

We've just set up a hostname record, which tells the DNS server that any request to `anything.slayercafe.com` should go to the `slayercafe.com` server. This will be useful later because WordPress MU will use this functionality to offer users `myname.slayercafe.com` blogs.

If you're not using cPanel hosting, you may need to email your host to ask them to set up the wildcard subdomains for you.

One last thing—wildcards and Apache

The wildcard subdomains feature is a nice one, but it's not much of a use if our web server doesn't know what to do with it. So, we've got one more thing to do. We can then get on with installing WordPress MU, I promise!

1. You'll need to edit your `httpd.conf` file. If you can't access this file (many shared hosting accounts don't allow you to edit it), then you'll need to open a support ticket with your host.

2. If you wish your `httpd.conf` file to look something like the following, replace `123.123.123.123` with the IP address of your site, and replace `CPANEL_USERNAME` and `YOURDOMAIN.com` with your username and domain name respectively.

```
<VirtualHost 123.123.123.123>
DocumentRoot /home/CPANEL_USERNAME/public_html
BytesLog domlogs/YOURDOMAIN.com-bytes_log
User CPANEL_USERNAME
Group CPANEL_USERNAME
ServerAlias YOURDOMAIN.com *.YOURDOMAIN.com
ServerName www.YOURDOMAIN.com
CustomLog domlogs/YOURDOMAIN.com combined
</VirtualHost>
```

3. If you already have subdomains set up on your site, you will need to add this new `VirtualHost` entry after those subdomains.

What just happened?

We've just set up a new virtual host in Apache. Virtual hosts are used so that you can run more than one site on a single web server. They can be used to host multiple domains, or in this case, subdomains. The `VirtualHosts` file tells Apache to accept connections from people looking for `anysite.slayercafe.com` and directs them to the folder where the main `slayercafe.com` site is stored. Apache reads the `http_host` header and passes that information to WordPress MU, which then serves up the correct site.

Not using cPanel?

If you're not using cPanel and are having difficulty with any of the steps listed so far, I'd recommend you look at the documentation provided by your web host. If you choose one of the hosts mentioned in Chapter 1, then WordPress MU should run well and features such as wildcard subdomains should be supported. However, in some cases you may need to raise a support ticket to get certain features turned on.

Pop quiz – subdomains

1. Wildcard subdomains are useful because:
   a) They're more exciting than tame subdomains.
   b) They allow `anything.mydomain.com` to work as a valid address for the blog network.
   c) WordPress MU won't work at all without them.
   d) They stop you needing to buy a new domain name for each blog.

2. The `httpd.conf` file:
   a) Contains information Apache uses to display the right pages for each request, and allows pretty/SEO-friendly URLs.
   b) Can be used to make Apache serve several different sites from one server.
   c) Is often not editable on shared hosting, so if changes are needed you may have to contact the host to ask them to do it.
   d) All of the above.

   Answers: 1) b, 2) d

Installing WordPress MU

Good news! We're ready to set up WordPress MU. Fortunately, the WordPress MU setup process is nice and easy. We've done the hardest part—getting the server ready.

Time for action – getting WordPress MU up and running

The installation process for WordPress MU has been designed to be user-friendly. Therefore, as long as you have the database connection information we created earlier in this chapter, the installation should go quite smoothly.

1. Download the latest version of WordPress MU from `http://mu.wordpress.org/download/`.

2. Open the archive file and extract the contents of the `wordpress-mu` folder to the `www` folder in your `WAMP` directory.

3. Use your favorite FTP client to upload the contents of the `www` folder to the document root folder on your live server. On most servers the `root` folder will be called either `www` or `public_html`.

4. Browse to the live version of your site—in our case `slayercafe.com`. You should see a page like the following:

WordPressµ

Installing WordPress µ

Welcome to WordPress µ. I will help you install this software by asking you a few questions and asking that you change the permissions on a few directories so I can create configuration files and make a directory to store all your uploaded files.

If you have installed the single-blog version of WordPress before, please note that the WordPress µ installer is different and trying to create the configuration file wp-config.php youself may result in a broken site. It's much easier to use this installer to get the job done.

What do I need?

- Access to your server to change directory permissions. This can be done through ssh or ftp for example.
- A valid email where your password and administrative emails will be sent.
- An empty MySQL database. Tables are prefixed with wp_ which may conflict with an existing WordPress install.
- Wildcard dns records if you're going to use the virtual host functionality. Check the README for further details.

Warning!

One or more of the directories must be made writeable by the webserver. You will be reminded to reset the permissions at the end of the install.
Please chmod 777 "directory-name" or chown that directory to the user the web server runs as (usually nobody, apache, or www-data)
Refresh this page when you're done!

Quick fix:
`chmod 777 /home/slayers/public_html /home/slayers/public_html/wp-content/`

If there are any warnings about file permissions, you can fix these using your FTP client. Right-click on the folders mentioned in the Quick fix section and select **File Attributes**. In the screen that appears, enter **777** in the **Numeric value** box. If you don't see any warnings, skip to step six.

5. Refresh the page once you're done setting attributes.

6. Enter your database connection details in the relevant boxes. In most cases, the database host will be **localhost**. If it is different on your web server, you will most likely have been told the name of the server when you created your database.

7. The server address on your live server will be your domain name— slayercafe.com in our case. On your local server it will be localhost.localdomain.

8. Make a note of the password that appears on the next page.

9. If you had to set permissions for any folders in step four, use the same process to change those permissions to 755.

10. Click **Log In** and you will be presented with the WordPress MU admin page.

11. Repeat step four with the other version of your site.

So, if you've just worked through the "live" version, finish the install on the local server too.

What just happened?

You've just taken the first steps towards running your blog network empire! At the moment, there's just the main site and the admin panel, but it's a solid foundation for us to build on. However, there are a few more things we need to do. First, change the admin password to something more memorable.

Changing the admin password

The default admin password is a random set of letters and numbers, which is secure, but not very memorable. Rather than writing it down and leaving it lying around where anyone could see it, we should change it to something equally secure, but more meaningful so that we can remember it.

Time for action – changing the admin password

Follow the steps mentioned next to change the admin password.

1. Go to the **Admin** link at the top of the screen. Scroll to the bottom of the page and enter your new password.

2. Pay attention to the strength indicator. It can be very useful in helping you pick a good password.

New
Password

●●●●●●●●●●●   If you would like to change the password type a new one.
Otherwise leave this blank.

●●●●●●●●●●●   Type your new password again.

Strong   Hint: Your password should be at least
seven characters long. To make it stronger,
use upper and lower case letters, numbers and symbols like ! " ? $ % ^ &).

3. When you've found a good password, click **Update Profile** at the bottom of the page.

Letting people register

You will most likely want to create some test accounts to explore the various features of WordPress MU, and get an idea of the differences between an admin account and a normal user account. Therefore, the next thing we should do is enable registrations. Once we're finished testing the site, we can turn off the registration option again until we are ready to accept new users.

Time for action – enabling registrations

Follow the steps mentioned next to enable registrations:

1. Expand the **Site Admin** side panel and click on **options**.

2. Under **Allow new registrations**, select the radio button that says **Enabled Blogs and user accounts can be created**.

3. Scroll down and click **Update Options**.

What just happened?

By now you should be getting a feel for the WordPress MU admin panel. It's a lot like the traditional WordPress admin panel, just with a few more options. We've temporarily turned on registrations for both new users and new blogs. We will be changing this option later, but for now this will allow us to test the registration process to make sure everything is working smoothly.

Testing your site

Let's make sure that everything is working. Go to the front page of the site; it should look something like the following:

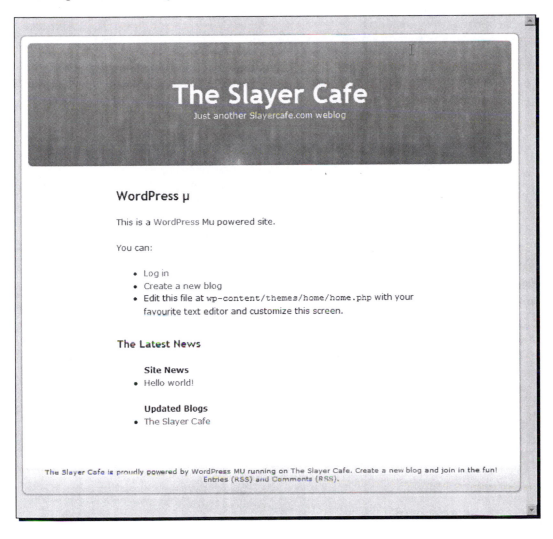

This is the page that new users will see when they visit your domain. It doesn't look like much yet, but it is the beginning of a blog network. We will install a new theme and start adding new features as we work through the book.

Time for action – creating a new user

For now, let's try making a new user and a new blog.

1. If you're not already logged out, click **Log Out** on the front page of the site.

2. On the front page of the site, click **create new blog**.

3. Enter a username and an email address. Leave **Gimme a blog!** ticked, and click **Next**.

4. Choose the subdomain you want, give your blog a title, and click **Sign Up**.

5. If everything goes well, you should get an email within a few minutes, and clicking the link in the email should send you to a confirmation page showing your username and password.

If your signup didn't work

If you don't receive the signup confirmation email, check the email settings in your WordPress MU control panel. If you get the email, but the link doesn't work, then the problem lies with the subdomains setting. A good place to look for advice when it comes to setting up WordPress MU is the official forums, which can be found at `http://mu.wordpress.org/forums`.

Have a go hero – doing more with the thing

In this chapter we set up a bare-bones install of WordPress MU. Before we start expanding it, why not familiarize yourself with a few of the features. Make some posts on the front page, and perhaps create a few fake users and blogs to populate the site a little. Try adding some new links to some of the blogs or uploading some videos.

Summary

This chapter involved a lot of preparation and server setup work. So, give yourself a pat on the back. You've got the hard work out of the way, and now you can focus on the more exciting parts of building your blog network empire.

Specifically, we covered setting up a local server (and what each part of the server is for), creating wildcard DNS entries in order to offer attractive, easy-to-remember blog URLs to your users, creating a database for WordPress MU, and setting up WordPress MU itself (the most important part!).

We also looked briefly at the control panel and some of the options in it—we will explore that in greater depth in later chapters.

Now that we've got a working blog network, it's time to spruce it up a little bit. In Chapter 3 we will look at customizing the appearance of the site—from installing new themes to making the front page more exciting and informative.

3
Customizing the Appearance of Your Site

In the previous chapter we set up a clean install of WordPress MU, which would allow your users to set up their own blogs. However, it doesn't really do anything else. The front page is pretty boring, and there isn't all that much to link the individual blogs together. In this chapter we will take the first steps towards rectifying that.

In this chapter, we will cover the following:

- Changing the default theme to something more appealing
- Tweaking the theme to make it work with WordPress MU
- Choosing plugins that will make the site look more like a community
- Adding some community features to the front page

Let's get started!

Picking out a theme

The WordPress community is full of skilled designers, and there are thousands of themes available for you to choose from. There are some good premium themes. There are also some generous people that offer their themes for free, while others offer their themes under various licenses such as the Creative Commons or GPL licenses.

A good starting point when searching for themes is the WordPress site `http://wordpress.org/extend/themes/`. There are lots of other good sites, a few of which are listed next:

- `http://www.themelab.com/free-wordpress-themes/`

- `http://www.skinpress.com/`

- `http://wpmudev.org/`

In general, WordPress themes do work with WordPress MU. However, it is worth searching for a WordPress MU-specific version of a theme, as it may have some extra WordPress MU-specific features.

Be sure to read the license file for any theme you are planning to use, and make sure you comply with the terms of the license. Usually, all that is required is a link back to the theme designer in the footer of your site, which is a very small price to pay for a quality theme.

`SlayerCafe.com` will use a clean, simple theme called Blue Zinfandel. This is because we want the page to load quickly. We also want to keep the page clean, leaving plenty of room for the information we will be adding as the site is developed. Our target audience—vampire Slayers and their Watchers—is a very diverse group. They could be accessing the site from anywhere in the world and could be using very old hardware or slow connections, so a minimalistic site is a good idea.

Your target audience could be very different—for example actors wishing to promote their latest movies or computer gamers wanting to talk about their hobby. Those groups of people are likely to have fast computers, big monitors, and fast broadband connections, so a more graphically intensive theme may appeal to them.

As usual, any instructions given in this chapter assume you are extracting files to your local copy of the site, and editing files on your local machine before testing them, and then uploading them to your web server. If you need to do anything in the admin panel, you'll need to run through the steps twice—once locally and once on the server.

Installing your new theme

Installing themes in WordPress MU is fairly similar to installing them in plain old WordPress. The administrator of the site can control which themes are available for users to activate. They have the permission to set the default theme that will be used for the main site and will be switched on for all user blogs. You can have more than one theme installed and allow users to swap between themes as they wish.

Time for action – installing a new theme

I've chosen a pack of themes from WPMUDev.org and will offer visitors the choice of several different themes from the pack. We should pick a nice, clean looking theme for the front page, as eventually there will be a lot of information on there.

1. Choose the themes you would like to use (you can have more than one theme available at a time), download them, and extract the files to the /wp-content/themes folder on your local server.

2. If you plan to make the home page theme available to your users, make a copy of it in another directory. For example, the SlayerCafe site uses a theme called Blue Zinfandel. We will call the user's version of the theme Blue User.

3. Open the Style.css file in the Blue-User folder. At the start of the file is a line saying **Theme Name: Blue Zinfandel Enhanced**. Change the line to say **Theme Name: Blue User**— don't touch any other text in the file.

4. For each theme, upload the theme's folder (and any subdirectories) to /wp-content/themes on your web server using your FTP client.

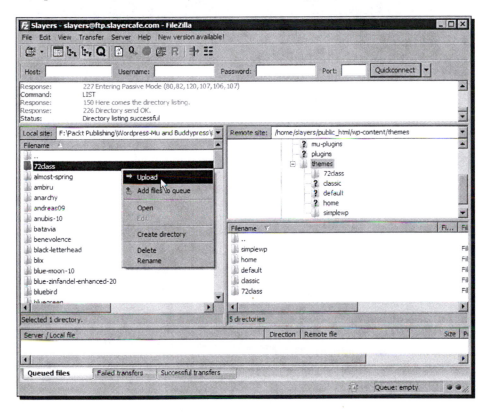

5. Go to the admin panel and select **Themes** from the **Site Admin** menu. Check **Yes** for those themes you want to let your users have access to (leave the option set to **No** if you do not want to make the theme available to your users), and then click **Update Themes**.

Hi admin! You're logged in as a site administrator.

Site Themes

Disable themes site-wide. You can enable themes on a blog by blog basis.

Active	Theme	Version	Description
⦿ Yes ◯ No	**72 Class**		Minimalist yet modern and beautifully executed.
⦿ Yes ◯ No	**Almost Spring**	1.0	Light and simple spring cleaning.
⦿ Yes ◯ No	**Ambiru**	1.0	A mellow one-column theme with a customizable header.

6. Now go to **Appearance** and select **Themes**. Click on the theme you would like to enable and then click **Activate theme** on the preview pane.

The Slayer Cafe — Visit site

New Post ▼

Hi admin! You're logged in as a site administrator.

Dashboard

Site Admin
Admin
Blogs
Users
Themes
Options
Upgrade

Posts
Edit
Add New
Tags
Categories

Manage Themes

Administrator: new themes must be activated in the Themes Admin page before they appear here.

Current Theme

Blue Zinfandel Enhanced 2.0 by Brian Gardner

Very modern, and kinda cool.

Available Themes

7. If you go to the blog network's home page, you should see the new theme in action.

Why two copies of the main theme?

You may be wondering why we are making a copy of the Blue Zinfandel theme. Well, we want to keep a fairly uniform look across the whole site, but there are some things that we won't want to display on our users' blogs, and we can't use widgets for all of the changes. So, we will use a heavily customized version of Blue Zinfandel for our home page; this version will have lots of extra features enabled, such as sitewide recent posts and comments. The Blue User version of the theme will have fewer edits by default, and our users can add extra features via widgets to customize their blog's appearance to their liking.

What just happened?

We have installed some new themes and enabled them in the admin panel. When you are logged in as the administrator of the site, the theme that you enable becomes the theme used for the home page, just as it would if you were using standard WordPress.

We created a copy of the home page theme so that any customizations we make to the home page theme don't affect our users' blogs.

Styling the sign-up page

If you try to create a new blog, you may find your sign-up page doesn't look very nice. Exactly how it looks will depend on the theme that you choose. The theme we're using on `SlayerCafe.com` has three columns. Also, the sign-up text should appear in the middle column, but it actually spreads across the whole page as you can see in the next screenshot. Fortunately, this is easy to fix.

Time for action – editing your theme

1. Open the `Style.css` file contained in the folder for the theme you are using.

2. Look for an entry called `#content`.

3. After that entry, add the following code:

```
.mu_register {
Width: 350px;
}
```

4. Upload your changes and revisit the sign-up page. If it works, you should see something like the following:

What just happened?

The main part of the sign-up page has its layout dictated by a CSS class called `content`. In the `content` class is an attribute called `widecolumn`. This attribute exists in the default WordPress theme but is missing from most other themes, so we needed to add it again by editing the CSS file. For those who are not familiar with **CSS**, it stands for **Cascading Style Sheets** and is used to style web pages. Instead of setting the appearance of every single element on your page individually—using old-fashioned HTML tags such as `<b>`, `<i>`, and `<font>`—you can use CSS to add styles to all instances of a specific element on a page, for example to ensure that all text surrounded by `<h1>` tags is colored blue and underlined.

You can also make your own CSS classes such as content, or leftSidebar, and set styles for those so that a link in the left sidebar of a page would have a different appearance than a link in a blog post. Be careful to choose unique names for your styles and comment the stylesheet so that you can easily identify the changes you have made. This makes it easy to maintain a consistent, professional look across all pages of your site. You can read more about CSS on the W3C site http://www.w3.org/Style/CSS/learning.

While there is some PHP inside many of the theme files, you can make extensive changes to the layout of your site without knowing a lot of PHP. Most of the WordPress MU functions are very clearly named, so you should be able to style your pages by leaving the functions in place and surrounding them with markup to achieve the desired result.

Does your sign-up page still look wrong and you are not able to see the content attribute?

If your sign-up page still looks wrong, there are a few things you can do. If you are not able to see the content attribute, look for the attribute that looks like it does the same job (is responsible for the styling of the main part of the page), make a copy of it, and call the copy #content. Then, add the styling information for the widecolumn attribute.

If you're still having issues, you may need to make some bigger changes to the CSS or you could edit the WP-Signup.php page directly. However, this isn't recommended as the sign-up page may change in future WordPress MU updates, and you could lose your changes during an upgrade.

Have a go hero – it's time to style

One of the best things about CSS is that it makes it easy to change a site's styling. If there's something you don't like about your chosen theme, try to change it. Perhaps you want links to be in different colors, or underlined, or perhaps you don't like the header font. Things such as these should be easy to change just by editing the CSS file.

Again, if you aren't sure where to begin, check the following resources for more information about CSS:

- http://www.w3.org/Style/CSS/learning
- http://codex.wordpress.org/CSS
- http://tamba2.org.uk/wordpress/graphicalcss/

Much of the layout will be handled by the other theme files. We'll look at those later. When possible, it is best to stick to editing theme files rather than files that belong to WordPress MU itself, as your theme files will not be touched when you upgrade WordPress MU itself.

Setting the theme for your users' blogs

When you change the home page theme, this does not change the theme used on any blogs that your users will create. To keep a consistent look across the whole site, we may want to change this.

Time for action – changing the default blog theme

Follow the steps mentioned next to change the default blog theme:

1. Download the New Blog Defaults plugin from `http://wpmudev.org/project/New-Blog-Defaults`.

2. Place the `cets_blog_defaults.php` file in your `/wp-content/plugins` folder.

3. Activate the plugin by opening the **Plugins** section of the WordPress MU admin panel.

4. Now go to **Site Admin | New Blog Defaults**. You should see a page with a lot of options.

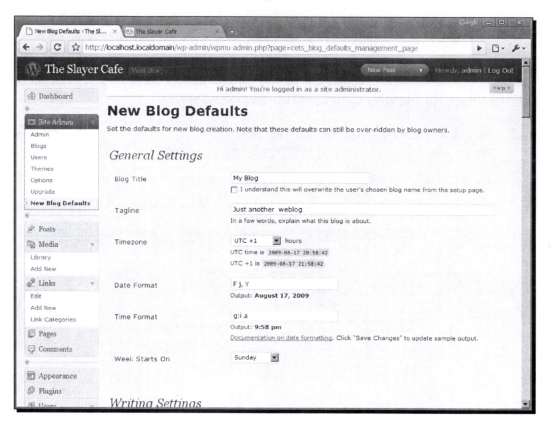

For now, the option we are interested in is **Default Theme**, which is at the bottom of the page. Select the theme **Blue User** and click **Save Changes**.

What just happened?

Congratulations, you've just installed your first plugin! This plugin allows you to set some basic default options to ensure that everyone who creates a blog on your site gets exactly the right look and feel. You can find plugins that will allow you to do almost anything you can imagine with WordPress MU, so be prepared to add many more plugins as your site evolves.

Customizing your home page

Now that we have a theme that we like, we can start building on it to make the site a little more interesting. In this section we will cover the following:

- Adding a sign-up button at the top of the page
- Adding a featured posts section to the main column of the blog
- Adding feeds for recent comments and new posts
- Displaying statistics such as the number of users online/number of blogs created

Time for action – making a sign-up button

The sign-up link on our chosen theme isn't exactly prominent. At first glance, new users may think that the site is private and that they can't join without contacting the administrator. While we do want to have some control over who joins `SlayerCafe.com`, we don't want to discourage people from applying. After all, the more people who join the fight against the vampires, the better.

Let's place a register link at the top of the screen where people can see it:

1. Open the `header.php` file for the theme that you are using for your home page. You will find the following piece of code:

   ```
   <div id="navbar">
           <ul>
   <li><a href="<?php echo get_settings('home'); ?>">
   <?php _e('Home');?></a></li>
   ```

2. Add in a sign-up link, along with a **Log In** and **Log Out** link.

   ```
   <li><?php wp_loginout(); ?></li>
   <li><?php wp_register(' ' , ' '); ?></li>
   ```

3. Log in to the admin panel, go to **Site Admin | Options**, and check the **Enabled Blogs and user accounts can be created** option. Then scroll down and click **Update Options**.

4. While you're on that page, let's update the tagline to make it something more exciting than "Just another xyz blog"—SlayerCafe is much more than that. You could have a tagline something like "Uniting Slayers in the fight against vampires and demons!"

5. Visit your site. If you are logged in, you should see a link to the admin panel; if you are not logged in, you should see a registration link as shown in the next screenshot:

What just happened?

We have altered our blog header so that it shows the right links to each viewer. If someone is logged in, they will be presented with the option to log out. If someone is not logged in, they will be invited to either log in or register.

If you want to make this link more noticeable, you could change it into an image or add some CSS styling to it in order to draw the attention of your visitors.

Featured posts

A lot of authors are inspired by the thought of people reading their work, so why not reward your best members by promoting their posts on the front page? This will make your blog network look more interesting as the content on the front page will change frequently and will usually contain interesting, high-quality posts. One way to accomplish this is by using the Featured Posts plugin.

Time for action – featured posts

To add the featured posts to the home page, we will use the Featured Posts plugin available at `http://wpmudev.org/project/Featured-Posts`.

1. Extract the plugin to the `/wp-content/plugins` directory.

2. Open `featured-posts.php` and look for the line that says `$featured_blogs = array(1,2);`. Replace the values in the bracket with the ID of the blogs you would like to feature—for example blogs owned by your fellow administrators. If you don't know the blog IDs, you can find them by looking at **Site Admin | Blogs**:

3. Upload the plugin to your site's `/wp-content/plugins` directory.

4. Go to **Site Admin | Options** in the admin panel, and enable plugins (they are turned off by default).

5. Now go to the **Plugins** section of the admin panel, look for the Featured Post plugin, and click **Activate**.

6. Open the `home.php` file for the theme you are using on the main site. Inside the main content div (in our case `<div id="contentmiddle">`), add the following line:

```
<h1>Featured Post:</h1><?php featured_posts(); ?>
```

7. You should now see a random post from one of the featured users on your home page.

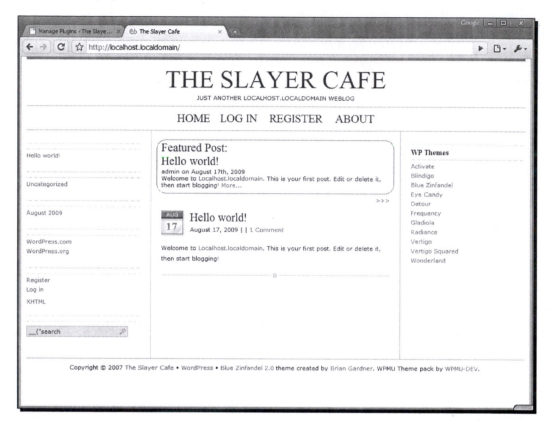

What just happened?

As I hinted at earlier in the chapter, you've just installed another plugin! This particular plugin pulls up a list of blog posts by the users you added to the "featured" list (the array in the plugin code), and then picks a post at random that is displayed by calling the `featured_posts()` function.

Have a go hero – styling the featured post

You may have noticed that the featured post looks slightly different than the normal posts on the front page, but not enough to make it noticeable. We need to edit `featured-posts.php`, which contains the code that dictates how the featured post section should look. Near the bottom of the code is a section with a comment saying "You should edit this to match your theme".

```
//Lets Output the Post - You Should Edit This To Match YOUR Theme
?>
    <div class="entry">
    <div class="entrytitle">
    <h1><a href="<?php echo $permalink; ?>" rel="bookmark" title="Link
to <?php echo $featured_post->post_title; ?>"><?php echo $featured_
post->post_title; ?></a></h1>
    <div class="endate"><?php echo $post_author; ?> on <?php echo
date('F jS, Y', strtotime($featured_post->post_date)); ?></div>
    </div>

    <div class="entrybody">
    <?php echo $summary; ?><a href="<?php echo $permalink; ?>"
rel="bookmark" title="Link to <?php echo $featured_post->post_title;
?>">More...</a>
    </div>
```

Try changing some of the layout markup in that section. Perhaps you could make the fonts bigger, change the background color, or underline the title to draw people's attention to it.

For example, to change the background color, change the `<div>` tag to `<div class="entry" style="background-color:#a8a8a8" >`. This makes the featured post area stand out from the rest of the page:

Showing off your statistics

Once you have built up a large user base, you may want to show off how popular the site is by showing how many bloggers are part of the community and how many blogs they are running.

Time for action – simple stats

1. Open the `r_sidebar.php` for the home page theme.

2. At the point where you would like the stats to appear—above the themes list in our case—insert the following code:

```
<li id="Stats">
<h2>Site Stats</h2>
<ul>
<li><?php
$stats = get_sitestats();
echo "SlayerCafe.com currently has
<b>".$stats[ 'blogs' ]."
</b> blogs and
<b>".$stats[ 'users' ]."
</b> users."; ?></li>
<li><?php include('vonline.php') ?></li>
</ul>
```

3. You can download the `vonline.php` file from `http://lesleyharrison.wordpress.com/2009/09/09/simple-stats-visitors-online/`.

4. Visit your blog, and you should see something like the following screenshot in the right sidebar:

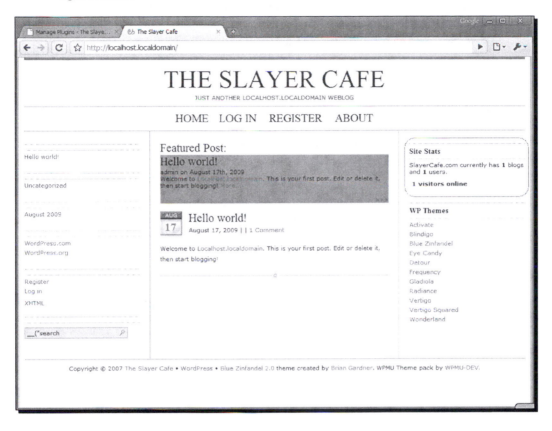

What just happened?

We've used a built-in WordPress MU function to get some information about the number of blogs and the number of users that the site has. We're then displaying that information in the sidebar of the main site. If you wish, you can add this code to the themes that you've made available to your users as well, so the site stats are visible on their blogs. You could include this information anywhere. If you wanted to make a statistics page or put the statistics in the footer of each page, all you need to do is edit the relevant theme file.

Have a go hero – adding extra stats

You can display more information in the sidebar if you wish. Take a look at wpmu-functions.php—there are a lot of useful functions in that file. Try experimenting with some of them to see what information you can pull from WordPress MU.

Wordpress MU has a lot of built-in functions. Many of the most interesting and useful ones can be found in the wpmu-functions.php file. There are functions for getting information about individual users, recently updated blogs, the most active blogs, and more. You can learn more about wpmu-functions.php by visiting the WordPress Codex at http://codex.wordpress.org/WPMU_Functions.

You can also include information from other scripts in your templates—for example, look for a simple script that will track the number of visitors on your site and try including that information in the sidebar.

Showing current online visitors

You can see an example of a script that will show your current online visitors in the Beginner's Guide section at http://lesleyharrison.wordpress.com. When you are including scripts in a template, be sure to use the absolute path rather than the relative path to the file. For example, if your file is in a folder called scripts in the root of the site, then the path should be <?php include(ABSPATH . '/scripts/vonline.php'); ?> if.

Pop quiz – doing the thing

1. The wpmu-functions.php file contains:

    a) The markup that tells WordPress MU how pages should look.

    b) Configuration information that tells the server how Apache and PHP should run.

    c) Useful functions webmasters may want to use in order to get information about their WP-MU site.

    d) Functions used by WordPress MU in its day-to-day operation.

2. WordPress MU themes:

    a) Contain CSS and HTML used to describe how the site is displayed.

    b) Are very different to WordPress themes—only themes made specifically for WordPress MU will work.

    c) Require extensive knowledge of PHP to edit.

Answers: (1) c , (2) a

Displaying recent posts and comments

Displaying information about how many users and blogs you have is useful, but it would make life much easier for your visitors if they could quickly and easily navigate to those blogs.

There are a few ways you can do this. One way is to offer a list of all users' blogs in the sidebar of the main site. There is a widget called List Blogs Widget, available on the WordPress MU site, which will do this for you. This may be a good idea if you are planning on running a small WordPress MU site that will have only a few users—perhaps a site for your local parish, or even a school blog network where teachers could post updates for parents.

However, in the case of `SlayerCafe.com`, we are expecting a large number of blog registrations from Slayers, Watchers, and vampire hunters all over the world. So, we need another way to offer content to our visitors.

Time for action – displaying the most active blogs

Rather than displaying all the blogs on the site, we will display the most recently updated ones using a plugin called AHP Sitewide Recent Posts, available at `http://wpmudev.org/project/AHP-Sitewide-Recent-Posts-for-WPMU`.

1. Download the plugin and extract it to your `/wp-content/plugins` folder. You may want to rename it to something more recognizable than the default name—for example, `recent_posts.php`.

2. Upload the plugin to your web server and enable it in your admin panel.

3. Open the `r_sidebar.php` file for the main site's theme.

4. Add the following code where you want the recent posts to appear. In our case we replaced the list of available themes with it.

```
<h2>Recent User Posts</h2>
<ul>
        <li><?php ahp_recent_posts(5, 30);  ?></li>
</ul>
```

5. Upload the changes. You should see a list of recent posts in the sidebar, as shown in the following screenshot:

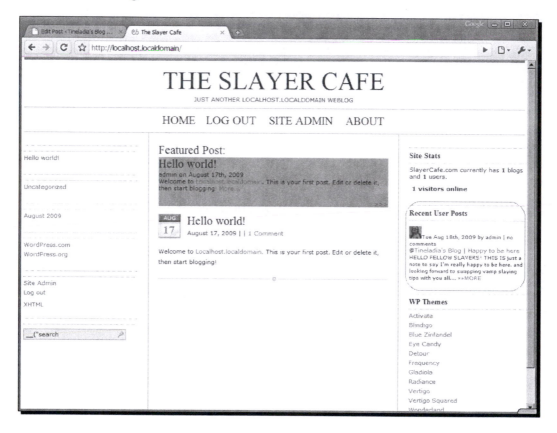

What just happened?

We installed the AHP Sitewide Recent Posts plugin and set it up using the default options. With those settings, the plugin shows the most recent posts (excluding the default **Hello World** posts made when a blog is created), along with the gravatar of the poster if they have one, and a link to the list of comments made on the posts (if there are any). The plugin also shows a very short excerpt from the post.

These settings are fine for most of the cases. However, you may want to change some of them—may be removing the excerpt or not showing the gravatar.

Customizing AHP Sitewide Recent Posts plugin

The recent posts plugin does not have an admin menu. You customize the menu by editing the plugin file directly. Most of the options are set by changing the `optmask` variable at the start of the plugin's code.

I'm quite happy with the appearance of the recent posts list on `SlayerCafe.com`, except for one thing. The first five words at the start of each blog post are displayed with all letters in upper case: I THINK THAT THIS LOOKS rather strange, so I think it should be turned off.

Time for action – tweaking the recent post display options

Follow the steps mentioned next to customize the recent post display options:

1. Open the PHP file containing the recent posts plugin code.

2. Scroll down until you find the line that has the `ahp_recent_posts` function.

3. Find the part that says `$optmask = 255` and change the number to `127`.

4. Save the file and reupload it.

5. Refresh the page. The posts should now display in the way intended by their author—no uppercase characters unless the author wanted them there.

What just happened?

We changed the setup of the AHP Sitewide Recent Posts plugin by setting the value of a bit mask. This isn't the first time we've worked with one, although it is the first time we've needed to use one for WordPress MU itself.

You may remember in Chapter 2 that we had to set some file attributes—the values we were setting there were also a form of bitmask.

With the AHP Sitewide Recent Posts plugin, the options are set using a variable called `$optmask`. It defaults to 255, which means that all the options are turned on. The available options are listed in the following table:

Bitmask	Display option
1	Show Gravatars
2	Show Post Date
4	Show Author Name
8	Show Comment Count
16	Show Blog Name
32	Show Post Name
64	Show Post Excerpt
128	Capitalize beginning of excerpt

To calculate the value to use in `optmask`, you can either start from zero and add up all the options you want switched on, or start from 255 and deduct the values you want to turn off (whichever is easier). For example, if you don't want to use gravatars, but want everything else left on, your `optmask` would be 254 (255-1).

There are some other options in the plugin file, which you can edit directly—for example if the gravatars are too small, change the `grav_size` variable. There are also variables to set the author prefix, the separator displayed before comments and posts, and the way the date is displayed. A list of options is shown in the following table:

Variable	Default setting
`$blog_prefix`	`"@"`
`$post_prefix`	`"	"`
`$auth_prefix`	`' by '`
`$com_prefix`	`'	'`
`$date_format`	`'D M jS, Y'`
`$grav_size`	24
`$debug`	0

Pop quiz – doing the thing

1. A bit mask is:

    a) A part of a mask.

    b) A mask worn by very small people.

    c) Something used to hide bits and bytes on your hard drive.

    d) Used to set options by adding or subtracting from a pattern of characters.

    Answer: d

Displaying Sitewide recent comments plugin

Sometimes the most interesting articles aren't the ones that have been posted most recently, so why not give our readers another view of the content on our site? Displaying recent comments is a good way to do this. Presumably, if someone feels that a post is worth commenting on, it must contain something interesting.

We will use the Sitewide recent comments plugin to enable this feature. You can download it from `http://wpmudev.org/project/Sitewide-recent-comments`.

Time for action – Sitewide recent comments

1. Download the plugin and extract it.

2. Upload the `sitewide_comments.php` file to your `/wp-content/plugins` folder and activate it in your WordPress MU admin panel.

3. Log in to phpMyAdmin, select your WordPress MU database, and select **SQL**.

4. Paste the contents of the file `CREATING-sitewide_table.txt` into the text box and click **ok**.

5. Once you have created this table, log in to your admin panel and enable the Sitewide recent comments plugin.

6. Open `r_sidebar.php` file for the theme that you want the plugin to apply to. In our case, we will be editing both the theme on the main site and the copy used on the individual user's blog.

7. At the point you would like to have a list of comments displayed, insert `<h2>Recent Comments</h2>`, followed by the code from `SAMPLE_CODE.php`.

> The code in `SAMPLE_CODE.php` needs a minor alteration, though. In the code, just after the bit that says `normal recent comment instead...}`, just add `?>`, or the desired screen may not be displayed.

On `SlayerCafe.com`, we added our Recent Comments code after the closing the `</ul>` tag that appears below the Site Stats code.

8. Find the comment that says **only for blogs 1 and 2**, and change the numbers in the preceding section of code to reflect the number of blogs you would like included. We would like to include comments on all blogs, so set the maximum number to `100`.

9. A few lines below this, change the number after `LIMIT` to `10`.

10. Remove the following lines of code:

```
if ($ach_blog_path == "/"){
  $ach_blog_path = "MainBlog";
}else{
  $ach_blog_path = trim($ach_blog_path, "/");
    $ach_blog_path .= "'s page ";
}
```

11. Replace those lines with the following:

```
$bname = get_blog_details($ach_blog_id)->blogname;
    $ach_blog_path = $bname;
$ach_blog_path = trim($ach_blog_path, ".");
```

12. Upload the changes. Make some comments on your test blogs and approve them in the admin panel.

13. View your blog. You should see a **Recent Comments** section that looks something like the following:

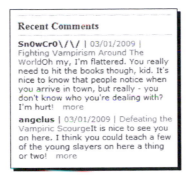

What just happened?

The Sitewide Recent Comments plugin creates a new table in your database, where it stores copies of all comments made after the plugin was installed. The plugin author chose to use this method because it would mean that the plugin would use fewer system resources during the day-to-day operation of the site.

WordPress MU creates a new set of tables for each blog that is hosted on a particular install. Ordinarily, to get a list of all comments on a site, you would have to query each blog's comment table. This would add a huge overhead to the site when you consider that the query is run every time a page with the recent comments code included is viewed, and there could be hundreds of blogs on the site.

When you are using this plugin, comments are copied into the plugin's `comments` table as they are created, which means one extra database action every time a comment is made. However, the saving is that the plugin has to call only one table to get a list of all the comments on the site.

We activated the plugin sitewide so that it would keep track of comments on all our users' blogs.

> **What about existing comments?**
>
> The plugin only adds new comments to its database. If you already have some comments on your blog, and you would like to see them copied over, you will need to add them to the database manually. To do this, use the `MySQL UNION` statement (`http://dev.mysql.com/doc/refman/5.0/en/union.html`) to get a list of all the comments in the blog, export the results in a suitable format such as a CSV file, and then import them into the new table.

The plugin display code

We made a few edits to the plugin's display code.

First, we changed the number of blogs to display comments from the default (blogs 1 and 2) to cover the first 99 blogs. At the moment, we don't have that many blogs on our site, but the code will still run and process all the blogs that it finds. We could initially set the number of blogs to 9999 to make sure that all users' blogs will be included. The LIMIT is the number of records returned by the query. We changed this value to 10—the maximum number of recent comments we want to display at a time.

The sample code that comes with the plugin is intended for sites where the users' blogs are hosted in subdirectories such as `http://www.slayercafe.com/victory`. As our site is set up so that the blogs are in subdomains (`victory.slayercafe.com`), the display code incorrectly states that all comments came from MainBlog.

We fixed this by removing the code that looks at the blog's URL to determine its name and by replacing it with a call to `get_blog_details`—a function found in `wp-functions.php`. We sent the ID of the blog to the function and asked it to return the name of the blog.

Does your blog use subdirectories?

If your blog uses subdirectories, you can use the sample code that comes with the plugin to show the short blog name. However, our edited version of the code will still work.

The `get_blog_details` function can be used to find out a lot about a blog from its ID. Check the WordPress Codex (`http://codex.wordpress.org`) for details on what the function can tell you.

Pop quiz – multiuser plugins

1. The `mu-plugins` folder:

    a) Contains all plugins used by your WordPress MU site.

    b) Is the folder used to store plugins written by the WordPress MU developers themselves.

    c) Is the folder used to store plugins you would like to have automatically activated on user blogs.

    d) Is no longer used in current versions of WordPress MU.

    Answer: c

Time for action – our improved home page

We are now displaying a lot more information on our home page, but it may not all be in the format you like. Take a look at the plugins and see if you can tweak the display to how you like it. Also, look at the Most Active Blogs plugin available at `http://wpmudev.org/ project/most-active-blogs`. Depending on the nature of your community, you may prefer that plugin to the recent posts that we are using.

Finally, look at the rest of the home page. In the sidebar, `SlayerCafe.com` still has some links to `WordPress.com` and some other sites. It's about time we changed these links to something more appropriate! Fortunately, this is easy to do through the admin panel, similar to the regular WordPress.

Other important points

While working through this chapter, if you have seen some error messages such as **Allowed memory size of X bytes exhausted** on your site, then you may need to make a change to your `php.ini` file.

Even today, many web hosts place very tight restrictions on the amount of memory available to PHP. Some hosts allow only 8 or 12 MB, which is not enough for WordPress MU.

If you are on shared hosting, you can change the PHP memory limit by opening your `.htaccess` file and adding a line that says `php_value memory_limit 24MB`.

If you run your own server, you can change the memory limit inside the `php.ini` file—this is probably found in the `/etc/php5/apache2` folder. You will need to restart Apache for the change to take effect.

WordPress MU uses a lot of memory, so you may need to set the value to be fairly high.

Summary

We have covered quite a lot in this chapter. We learned how to build on existing WordPress MU functionalities to display information about our site and use plugins to offer even more information to our users.

Specifically, we covered how to install new themes and change which ones are available to our users. We learned how to edit themes, to fix common issues with themes designed for WordPress instead of WordPress MU, and to change the look of a theme to better suit your site. We discussed how to display recent posts and comments on your home page and how to add a featured posts section. We also talked about using WordPress functions to get information about your blog, which can then be used to supply your visitors with interesting statistics.

We also recapped some common hosting issues such as the PHP memory limit, which can cause your blog to crash if you are on shared hosting or have a VPS that still has the default PHP settings.

Now that we've made our site more attractive to new users, we can give users the ability to customize their own blogs—the topic of the next chapter.

4
Letting Users Manage Their Blogs

In the previous chapter, we looked at customizing the front page of the blog network. Now it's time to consider giving our users some freedom to make their mark on their respective blogs.

In this chapter we will look at the following:

- User management of themes
- Plugins and widgets
- Restricting disk space usage
- Permissions and groups
- Limiting options on the user's admin panel
- How to let users have their own domain point to their blog

Let's get started!

User management basics

The default setup for WordPress MU is quite restrictive in terms of what it allows your site's users to do. For example, they have very limited storage space on their blog and they cannot upload images, videos, or audio files. We should change that and, while we're at it, make sure that our users don't accidentally disable any essential plugins or use the theme that is only intended for the main site.

Preparing the site for our users

Let's start with a look at the basic options given on the **Options** page in the site admin panel.

- Under **Banned Names**, add the names (with spaces between them, not commas) **support**, **webmaster**, **info**, **Dracula**, **council**, **watchers**, and **buffy**.
- Under **Banned Email Domains**, add **@thecrypt.com** and **@blooddrinkers.com** for now. We can add more options later.
- Make sure the **Images** and **Videos** options are ticked in the **Upload Media** section.
- Increase the **Blog upload space** to **50MB**.
- Change the **Upload File Types** to `jpg`, `jpeg`, `png`, `gif`, `mov`, `avi`, `pdf`, and `flv`. Change the **Max upload file size** to **3000KB**.
- Set the **Admin Notice Feed** to `http://slayercafe.com/feed/`.
- Leave the **Plugins** menu checked in the **Administration Settings | Menus** section.
- Click the **Update** option.

The site options page gives you a lot of control over the site even in its default state. We just saw a few of those options, but let's consider them in more depth.

Banned Names

We have added some extra names to the **Banned Names** section to prevent people from signing up with those names and tricking users into believing they work for the site. A few years ago, it was quite common for malicious attackers to create accounts named "SiteAdmin" or "Support" and then contact users asking for their login details. Many inexperienced site users would trust the person contacting them because they had an official sounding name, and they would willingly hand over their personal details. This kind of attack is known as **Social Engineering**.

Fortunately, most web services now have blocks in place to prevent people from signing up with a username such as "Admin". We've taken advantage of the built-in WordPress feature to do this.

Limited Email Registrations and Banned Email Domains

If your site is intended to be used by members of an educational institution or a specific company, you could put the school or company domain name in the **Limited Email Registrations** box to prevent outsiders from signing up.

SlayerCafe doesn't quite fit into this category. Anyone can apply to become a member, but only people who are actively involved in vampire hunting will be accepted. As an administrator will have to look over each application, the ideal scenario would be for only those people who are seriously interested in joining the site to be registering. One way to reduce "junk" registrations is to require the use of an ISP email address (or a personal domain).

Banning free email addresses is a major step, and one that could seriously reduce the number of legitimate registrations on your site. For this reason, I would not recommend it if you are planning on running a site that is aimed at a very wide audience. However, in the case of SlayerCafe, the target audience will appreciate the need to keep the site fairly private and to keep the load on the administrators to a minimum.

You can download a list of free email addresses to use as a starting point from `http://lesleyharrison.wordpress.com/2009/03/13/list-of-free-email-addresses-to-ban/`.

Media restrictions and upload space

By default, users are not allowed to upload any files. As the purpose of SlayerCafe is to allow Slayers to share information with each other, it makes sense to let users share images and videos.

Ten megabytes is not a lot of upload space, especially if the site's users will be posting photographs or videos. Of course, drive space is not infinite, so you will need to find the right balance between offering lots of features to your users and keeping your hosting costs down. One option is to offer a small amount of space to new users, and then sell upgraded membership packages that offer more space and fewer restrictions. Giving new members 50MB of upload space seems like a fair starting point.

The file types you would allow users to share are up to you. Most blog users will want to upload only .jpg, .gif, and perhaps .bmp or .png image files, along with .avi, .wmv, and .flv videos. If your site caters to a specific niche, say graphic designers, then you may want to allow the sharing of other file types such as .psd (Photoshop) files.

However, there are some file types that can be very dangerous and should not be allowed unless you are hosting a private site where all the members can trust each other. A few of the more dangerous extensions are listed in the following table.

File extension	Type
.exe	Executable program
.com	MS-DOS program
.pif	Short cut to an MS-DOS program
.bat	Batch file
.scr	Screen saver (could be an executable that has been renamed)
.zip	Compressed archive
.app	Mac application
.sh	Linux script
.bash	Linux script

The default value for **Max upload file size** is set to a little over 1MB. This is fine for images but may be too small for videos. Changing the limit to 3000KB should allow the posting of fairly short .flv files. The limit could be increased further if you expect people to upload a lot of videos. There are certain web sites such as YouTube and Dailymotion that offer unlimited space for videos and make it easy for users to embed their videos on other sites, so if your site is a public blog network, I would not anticipate many users uploading a video to their blog directly.

Of course, we will need to allow users to embed videos from external sites. Take a look at the *Have a go hero* section for a pointer to a plugin that will allow your users to post embedded video content.

Allowing bigger file uploads

If you decide to allow your users to upload files bigger than 3MB, you will need to edit your php.ini file to allow for the larger uploads. The settings you need to change are upload_max_filesize and post_max_size. Remember that in php.ini, 10MB is written as 10M (note the lack of the B).

Plugins

Finally, in the sitewide settings section we have left the option for users to manage their plugins enabled. We want to allow users some freedom when it comes to managing plugins. Plugins placed there will always be enabled and will be hidden from the plugin list shown to normal users.

Any optional plugins can be uploaded to the /wp-content/plugins folder. Those plugins will be visible to normal users who can activate or deactivate them at will.

Have a go hero – embedded videos

By default, WordPress MU has quite strict rules on what is allowed in posts. If you would like to allow your users to post videos, check out this plugin: http://wpmudev.org/project/Allow-Embedded-Videos. It is very easy to install and supports most popular video sites.

Customization options for your users

Many users like to customize their corner of the Web. If you would like to allow your users to change or edit their themes, then there is a plugin called Userthemes that you may find useful. The plugin is not without risks, however, and you may decide that a better option is to just offer your users a choice of several fixed themes instead.

Time for action – offering a selection of themes

We touched on the possibility of offering your users the choice of several themes in Chapter 3, but let's recap:

1. To offer multiple themes, just upload the themes you want to allow your users to activate to the `/wp-content/themes` folder.

2. In your admin panel, open the **Site Themes** section and make sure the themes you want your users to be able to use are set to **Yes**.

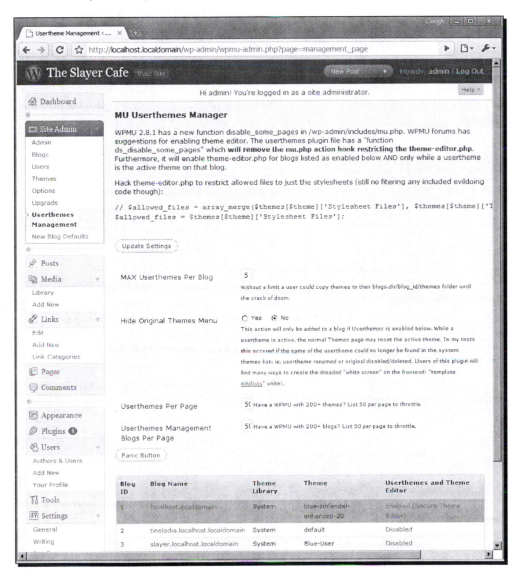

3. The theme used by the main site should be set to **No**.

4. The choices should be visible on the user's admin panel.

What just happened?

As we discussed in Chapter 3, it is possible to enable themes on a sitewide level so that our users can activate them if they wish.

On SlayerCafe, we ideally want our users to stick to the default theme (the copy we made of the theme used on the main site), but we have offered some choices for people who want to be different. The theme used by the home page is not offered as an option for our users because it is going to be heavily customized, and many of the changes are things that we want to appear only on the home page. In Chapter 3, we created a copy of the main blog theme that we will be offering to our users.

Some users may decide they like the default theme but want to make a few changes to it. It is possible to allow your users to edit themes, and we'll look at that next.

User editable themes

You can allow users to make a copy of one of the default themes and edit it by using the Userthemes Revisited plugin, which can be downloaded at `http://wpmudev.org/project/Userthemes-Revisited`.

Warning: Enabling the theme editor could put your site at risk!

The theme editor is disabled by default in WordPress MU for a very good reason. The theme editor is set up in order to allow you to put raw PHP code into theme files. This, combined with the way WordPress MU has been coded in order for all the blogs to be contained in one database, means that malicious users could do a lot of damage to your site if they were given access to the theme editor.

We will explore ways to reduce the risk in the *What Just Happened?* section, but you should be aware that the risk cannot be completely eliminated, and you should give theme editor access to only those users whom you trust completely.

Time for action – userthemes revisited

1. Download the edited version of userthemes revisited from
    `http://wpmudev.org/project/Userthemes-Revisited`.

2. Download the edited core files from `http://lesleyharrison.`
    `wordpress.com/2009/09/10/editing-userthemes-revisited/`.

3. Place `theme-editor.php` in the `/wp-admin` folder.

4. Place `mu.php` in `/wp-content/includes/`.

5. Upload the edited version of the plugin to your `/wp-content/plugins` folder.

6. Visit your site's admin panel, and enable the Userthemes Revisited plugin.

7. Go to **Site Admin | Userthemes Management** and enable user themes for
    one of your users as a test. Leave the other options as default for now.

8. Log in as the user you have just enabled theme access for. In the admin panel, under **Appearance | Userthemes**, they should see a page similar to this one:

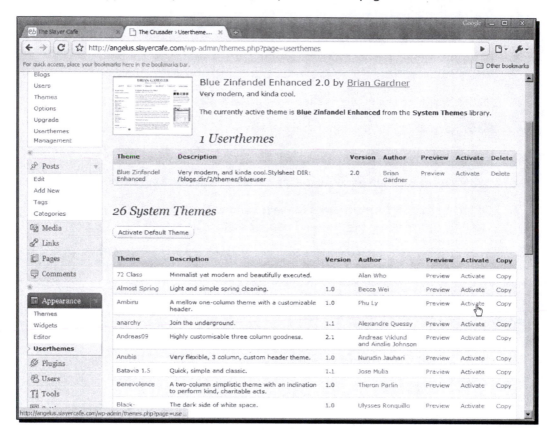

9. Once they have copied a theme, they should be able to edit it using the theme editor.

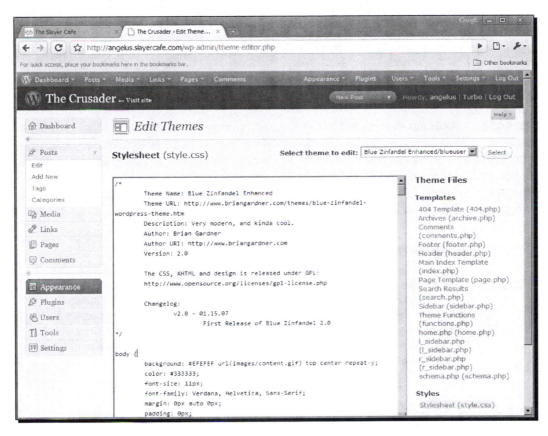

What just happened?

We have installed a plugin that allows users to make a copy of the original site theme inside their own blog folder and edit it.

The revised version of Userthemes Revisited has had some code commented out. This was code that told WordPress MU to allow editing of both PHP and CSS files. We changed that line to allow only CSS files to be edited.

If you wish to allow the editing of PHP files, just change that line back. (An explanation of the code that was changed can be found in the blog post linked in Step 1.) I would only recommend this on a very closed network of bloggers who are all trustworthy and all have a good knowledge of PHP!

The way we have set up the plugin, users can edit the `stylesheet.css` file but not any of the PHP files. If they try to edit those files, they will be shown an error message that says they are not allowed to edit PHP files.

To allow our users to easily get to the theme editor, we re-enabled the link to it using the Userthemes Revisited plugin. If a user has the ability to change theme files, clicking the link will take them to the theme editor. If they do not have that privilege, they will be shown an error message.

It should be noted that even plain CSS can be used for malicious purposes, so you should be careful who you give the ability to edit themes. If you have a fairly small member base, you could use the Userthemes Revisited plugin as a way to allow users to have unique themes, but you should require users to email you their new stylesheets so that you can look them over before uploading them, instead of letting them upload the file themselves. This is extra work for you, but it may be worthwhile in terms of security.

> **If the theme editor is not loading**
>
> If your `theme-editor.php` file is not loading, check the first few lines of the file for a line that says `wp_die( "The theme editor is disabled" );`. Comment that line to re-enable the theme editor. You can signify the start of a section you want to comment with the characters `/*` and the end with `*/`. If your comment is only one line long, then you can simply use the characters `//`. Everything after those characters, up until the end of the line, is treated as a comment.

User roles and admin panels

How much control you give your users will depend on the nature of the site you are building. With SlayerCafe, we do not want to let the majority of our users make major changes to the backend of their blogs. After all, the community will be catering to a very large, geographically separated community of vampire slayers. Even the Watchers Council has trouble keeping tabs on all of the Slayers in the world, and they have a Watcher for every Slayer. As a blog network is run by a small team, what hope do we have of knowing if every Slayer using the site can be trusted?

However, we do want to be able to give the moderator privileges to some of our most trusted users, and we may sell upgraded memberships to our users where premium members get access to more features. With moderator privileges, the most trustworthy Slayers can spend their downtime between fighting the forces of darkness doing some slightly less risky (and less exciting) fighting of spammers and the more mundane variety of troll. Should those Slayers ever be tempted by evil, we, as site admins, can rest assured that the damage they can do to SlayerCafe is minimal.

Time for action – setting user levels and changing the user's admin panel

Even the smallest of sites can benefit from having more than one person with the ability to carry out basic backend tasks. You may not want to give full admin power over to your users, but having someone who has moderator powers could well be beneficial.

Let's start by looking at admin duties and roles. The Role Manager plugin, which can be downloaded at `http://www.im-web-gefunden.de/wordpress-plugins/role-manager/`, is a good start.

1. Upload the Role Manager plugin to `/wp-content/plugins`.

2. Enable the plugin.

3. Go to Site **Admin | Blogs** and click **Edit** on one of your user's blogs, then fill in the name of your moderator in the **Add a new user** box, and set their role to be moderator.

4. You will need to repeat this step for each blog.

What just happened?

We have used the Role Manager plugin to create an account with limited admin privileges. Actually, the privileges shown in the preceding screenshot are not very limited at all, and I would not recommend giving that much power to your moderators unless you expect them to also be performing a tech support role on the site and trust them not to abuse their privileges. Remember that just because someone has been given some roles, it does not mean that they are permanent. They can be revoked, and we may need to remove someone's rights if they become possessed by demons, sired by a vampire, or turn to the dark side voluntarily.

A regular moderator account may grant the ability to edit posts and pages, and perhaps edit links, but not read private posts.

Have a go hero – creating new roles

The Role Manager plugin is very versatile. You can create new roles and new capabilities that you can assign to specific users.

This has several possible uses. You may want to give a very talented writer access to your main blog to post new content, but you may not want to allow them to change anything else. Set up a "writer" role for them, and then they can log in and make their own posts without you needing to worry about them doing anything else while they're there.

Or, you may want to give a programmer access to your site to tweak some plugins for you, but you don't want to allow them to edit any posts.

WordPress MU does already have some preconfigured roles, but by using the Role Manager plugin. you can personalize the roles to suit your site more closely.

Try setting up some new roles. If you plan on selling premium memberships to your site, think about the abilities you may not want people signed up as free users to have and create a limited access account for those users.

Roles and capabilities explained

As usual, one of the best places to read more about roles and capabilities is the WordPress Codex. WordPress has some pre-created roles—administrator, editor, author, contributor, and subscriber. These roles are a good starting point for assigning different capabilities. A contributor, for example, can publish posts but cannot edit users.

To learn more about the capabilities supported by WordPress MU, what they mean, and how these can be tied to different roles, visit `http://codex. wordpress.org/Roles_and_Capabilities`.

Once you've set up a new, limited role for new users, you can try making that role apply to all new users. We will cover how to upgrade paying users in Chapter 10. If you would like to restrict the privileges of new users, install the Default User Role plugin, which can be downloaded here: `http://wpmudev.org/project/Change-blog-administrator-role`.

Hiding the dashboard

By default, the first thing people see when they log in to the WordPress MU admin panel is the dashboard. This shows some useful information, but it also contains a lot of things that the average user would not be interested in. Plus, it takes a long time to load.

Let's disable the dashboard for our normal users as Slayers don't have time to be waiting around; they want to get posting, then slaying.

Time for action – hiding the dashboard

1. Download the 'Hide Dashboard plugin from `http://lesleyharrison. wordpress.com/2009/09/11/hiding-the-wordpress-mu-dashboard/`.

2. Upload the plugin and enable it in your admin file.

3. After you enable the plugin, you should see that the dashboard section is gone.

4. Try logging in as a user with restricted roles. The screen they are presented with should look nice and tidy.

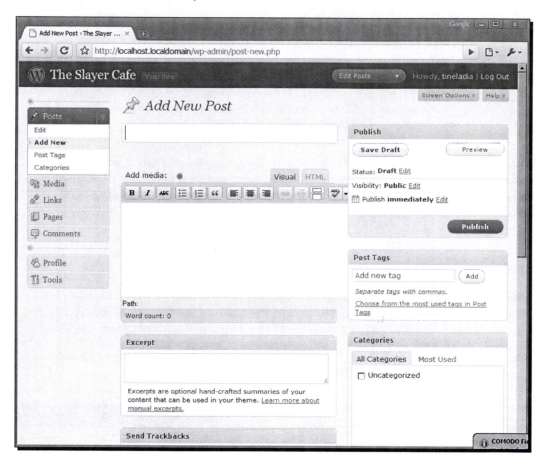

What just happened?

We have used a modified version of the Hide Dashboard plugin to hide the dashboard for all users. We checked the original code to see if the logged in user had the capability of `'level_10'`; this is the level that administrator accounts are set to.

With the original plugin, if the user was an administrator, the plugin would not run and the user would be shown the dashboard when they logged in to the admin panel. All other users would be redirected to the **Add New Post** page, which is the page they most likely wanted to see when they logged in. The modified version of the plugin runs for all users, including administrators.

If you want your site's administrators to see the dashboard, you can upload the original version of the plugin and take advantage of the Default User Role plugin mentioned earlier in this chapter to reduce the user level of your site's users.

More user options – privacy and using their own domain

Before we conclude this chapter, there are a couple of other plugins worth a mention. The first one, More Privacy Options, can be downloaded at `http://wpmudev.org/project/More-Privacy-Options`.

More Privacy Options is a fairly simple plugin to set up. It expands on the existing privacy options to allow users to determine who can and cannot read their posts. The administrator of the main site can also use the plugin to make sitewide changes such as setting all posts to be readable by members only.

The other plugin—WordPress MU Domain Mapping—can be used to allow members to have their own domain name point to their blog.

Time for action – domain mapping

1. Download the WordPress MU Domain Mapping plugin from `http://wordpress.org/extend/plugins/wordpress-mu-domain-mapping/`.

2. Upload the plugin file (`domain_mapping.php`) to the `/wp-content/mu-plugins` folder.

3. Check `/wp-content/` for a file called `Sunrise.php`.

4. If the file is not there, upload the one that came with the plugin.

5. If there is already a `Sunrise.php` file in the folder, compare the two and paste over any needed changes from the one that came with the plugin.

6. Open `wp-config.php` and uncomment the following line:

    ```
    define( 'SUNRISE', 'on' );
    ```

7. Go to **Tools | Domain mapping**, and you should see a message saying **Domain mapping database table created**.

8. Now your users should see a page that looks similar to the following:

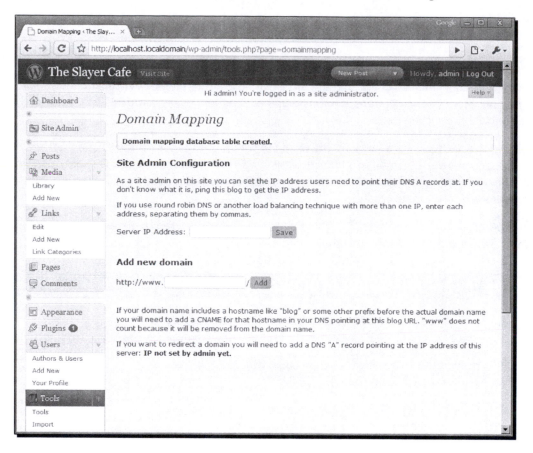

What just happened?

We have set up a Domain Mapping plugin that will allow our users to use their own domain name as the address for their blog. In its current state of development, the plugin will allow users to log in to their admin panel using their domain, but if they navigate to another part of the blog network, they will need to log in a second time.

The plugin works like this:

The user configures the nameservers of their domain so that it points to the blog network; so, Tineladia could buy a domain name and point it to SlayerCafe using a CNAME record.

When a visitor makes a request for Tineladia's domain name, your web server looks at the request and directs it to WordPress MU, which then checks the database and sees that the request was actually for `tineladia.slayercafe.com`.

So far, we have only installed the plugin. So, WordPress MU now knows what to do with a request for a specific domain name, but the server needs to be configured to pass the request on to WordPress MU.

Have a go hero – server setup for domains

How you handle the server-side configuration depends on the type of server you are using. If you are using a dedicated server or VPS where you have full control over your site, you can just edit your `Apache config` file to set up a wildcard server alias so that any requests for a site that haven't already been set up are directed to WordPress MU for it to determine what to do with them.

If you are using something such as cPanel, you will need to add each new domain individually using the `AddonDomains` function, and point the document-root to your WordPress MU install.

I suggest you write a help page on the main blog explaining to your users what they would need to do on their end to make their domain name point to their blog, and check the documentation of your host or server software to see if you need to make any changes.

Pop quiz – doing the thing

1. Capabilities are:

    a) Things that users can do; a role can have multiple capabilities.

    b) Jobs that a user has (for example, an administrator or editor).

    c) Biting, clawing, flying, and drinking blood.

2. Roles are:

    a) Tasks such as making blog posts or editing comments.

    b) A Slayer takes a test when she turns 16 and gets roles assigned based on the results of that test.

    c) Set only once and cannot be changed later.

    d) A quick way of assigning someone the ability to do certain things; a role can have several capabilities assigned to it.

3. The dashboard is:

   a) The admin panel for WordPress MU.

   b) The default front page of the admin panel, which contains a lot of information but can be slow to load, so some people choose to disable it.

   c) The front page of your blog.

   d) A training tool that Slayers use to improve their agility and speed.

   Answers: (1) a (c may technically be true, but not in the context of WordPress MU), (2) d, (3) b

A few things to consider

We have covered quite a few topics in this chapter, from giving your users almost full control over their individual blogs to locking the network down so that users have very few powers beyond making posts and moderating comments.

Which route you take depends on who your target audience is, how powerful your server is, how concerned you are about security, and the business plan you have for your site.

It may be safe, in a small workplace environment, to allow all your employees to edit the PHP code of your themes because you trust them not to abuse the privilege. Doing the same on a public blog network is almost as risky as posting the FTP details for the web site on a hacker's forum!

Allowing users to copy themes and edit stylesheets is less risky, but there are still some dangers to consider—CSS files can be used for XSS (Cross Site Scripting) attacks. Also, imagine that you have 1000 users and they all copied over 20 themes to their personal blog folders. You would find a lot of drive space eaten up very quickly.

Summary

We covered a lot of ways to offer new features to the users, and we also learned how to restrict access to certain powerful or dangerous features.

Specifically, we talked about how to allow users to select different themes and edit theme stylesheets. We also learned how to allow users to upload images and embed videos into their blog posts. We talked about the potential dangers of this and how to ensure that users cannot upload dangerous files.

We tidied up the admin panel so that users only see the things they need, and we set up a role system that gives different rights to new users compared to site staff.

Of course, our users should have some control over their own blogs, so we gave them the ability to restrict who can read their posts. We also allowed them to point their blog to its own domain name so that their blog is more personalized.

Additionally, we discussed some security concerns and server resource concerns that may arise from certain changes.

Finding the balance between giving users what they want and keeping the load on your server to a minimum is difficult, and it may take a little experimentation. Once your site is closer to being ready to launch, you could try doing a limited sign-up beta and experimenting with different permissions to get user feedback. We will discuss ways to limit signups in the next chapter and look at security in depth, along with a few other important site management techniques such as taking backups and fighting spammers.

5

Protecting Your Site

SlayerCafe aims to provide Vampire Slayers, Watchers, and talented demon hunters with a safe and friendly place to share advice and information. Ideally, SlayerCafe should be free of demonic spies, evil-doers, and trolls (of the Internet kind, not the mythical one).

One sad fact about the Internet is that hackers often target web sites "just because they are there". SlayerCafe faces danger on two fronts. Firstly, vampires may hire technomages to attack the site because they see it as a threat. And secondly, simply having a server connected to the Internet is an invitation to hackers who are looking for easy targets.

Our goal in this chapter is to protect the site from spies, spammers, and hackers. We want to make sure that only the people who belong on SlayerCafe can join, that the site is kept free of spam, and that the personal information of our members is well protected.

This chapter will also look at ways to make the site easier to administer—from automating backups to making it easier to roll out new changes to the existing blogs.

In this chapter we will:

- ◆ Protect our site from spam with reCAPTCHA and Bad Behavior
- ◆ Make some changes to the `.htaccess` file to keep known "baddies" away from our site
- ◆ Moderate new registrations or make the site invite-only
- ◆ Install some new admin tools to make our lives easier
- ◆ Set up an automatic backup feature

So let's get on with it...

Signing up for reCAPTCHA

Before you can set up reCAPTCHA on your site, you will need to sign up for an account at `recaptcha.net` and request some keys for your blog. The keys are free.

You can get a key from `https://admin.recaptcha.net/`. When prompted, enter the domain name you are using for the WordPress MU site—without the www, and tick the box that says **Enable this key on all domains (global key)**.

Make a note of the two keys, as you will need them later.

Stopping spam with reCAPTCHA and Bad Behavior

Two of the most useful spam-fighting plugins are reCAPTCHA and Bad Behavior. The reCAPTCHA plugin fights spam by making sure that the person entering the spam is a human, not a spam bot. The Bad Behavior plugin takes a different approach. It keeps a list of known spammers that it will block from commenting on, or accessing, your site.

Time for action – setting up reCAPTCHA

1. Download the reCAPTCHA plugin from `http://wordpress.org/extend/plugins/wp-recaptcha/`.

2. Extract the file and upload the `wp-recaptcha` folder to your `/wp-content/plugins` folder.

3. Move the file `wp-recaptcha.php` out of the `wp-recaptcha` folder so that it is inside the `plugins` folder.

4. Enable the plugin inside the **Site Admin** panel.

5. Go to **Site Admin | reCAPTCHA** and add your **Public Key** and **Private Key**.

6. Tick **Enable reCAPTCHA for comments**, **Hide reCAPTCHA for registered users who can Publish Posts**, and **Enable reCAPTCHA for registrations**.

7. Now, if you go to the registration page, you should see a CAPTCHA box at the bottom. You should also see one when you attempt to make a comment on a blog post.

What just happened?

We've just set up the reCAPTCHA plugin. This is an innovative CAPTCHA plugin with a twist. Every time someone enters your site and answers a CAPTCHA question correctly, they are helping with a global project to digitize old books. This way reCAPTCHA provides a useful service to webmasters for free and, at the same time, it's doing a great service by preserving old works of literature.

CAPTCHA actually stands for **Completely Automated Public Turing test to tell Computers and Humans Apart**. The aim of reCAPTCHA is to make a CAPTCHA that can be read by most humans but is too difficult for **OCR (Optical Character Recognition)** bots to correctly interpret.

CAPTCHAs work by presenting visitors with a question that can only be answered by a human. This could be a simple math problem, a piece of text to read, or something as easy as asking the visitor to "click on the picture of the cat". The answer to the question is simple enough that any human being should be able to answer it, but the question is presented in a way that makes it hard for a computer to tell what the answer should be.

Some CAPTCHAs can now be solved by spam programs—the battle against spam is a constant process and spammers are willing to create increasingly sophisticated methods of solving CAPTCHAs in order to continue their spamming endeavors.

The original Turing test was created by Alan Turing as a way to see if computers could actually think. The idea behind the test was to have a real human talk to a computer and another human being. After a long conversation, the human would be asked to identify which of the conversations had been with a computer. If they cannot identify the computer reliably over the course of several tests, then the computer has passed the Turing test.

So far, there is no computer program that has passed the test. Alan Turing predicts that machines capable of running a program that can pass the test will not be available until 2029. When a user who is not currently logged in goes to register a new blog or make a comment, they will be presented with a CAPTCHA that contains two words. The words have a wavy line drawn through them to make them harder for bots to read. Both of the words come from old books that have had digital copies made using a scanner, but still need to be converted into text format.

One of the words shown to the user is a control word; the correct answer to that word is already known. The other word is one that still needs to be translated from image to text. If the user gives the correct answer for the known word, it is assumed that they also answered the unknown word correctly. Of course, reCAPTCHA does not rely on just one answer for each unknown word. What if someone made a typing error when answering one of the words? Every word is offered up for solving several times and the answers are compared. If a large number of people agree on the answer to the unknown word, then the word is considered to be solved.

Can't see reCAPTCHA on comments?

If you can't see the reCAPTCHA box when you go to make a comment on a blog post, make sure you are logged out! We've set up the plugin so that our members don't have to worry about entering a CAPTCHA to make a comment—after all, we already know that they are real people, not bots.

Bad Behavior

Bad Behavior is a spam-fighting plugin that attacks the issue of comment spam from several different angles to ensure that as much spam as possible is blocked, while keeping false positives to an absolute minimum.

Let's set it up:

Time for action – setting up Bad Behavior

1. Download the plugin from `http://www.bad-behavior.ioerror.us/download/`.

2. Extract the files.

3. Upload the contents of the `bad-behavior` folder to `/wp-content/plugins`.

4. You should have several files whose names begin with "bad-behavior" in the plugins folder and then some more inside a folder called `bad-behavior`.

5. To take full advantage of the plugin, you will need an account with `http://www.projecthoneypot.org`.

6. Once you've registered with Project Honey Pot, go to **Services | Setup HTTP Blacklist** and request an **http:BL Access Key**.

7. Go to the plugins section of the **Site Admin** panel and activate Bad Behavior sitewide.

8. Next, go to **Settings | Bad Behavior** and add your access key under the **http:BL** section.

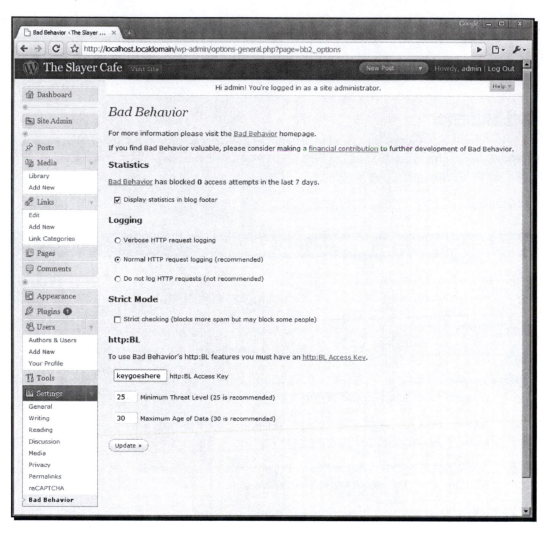

9. When a suspicious request is made to the site, the user will see the following:

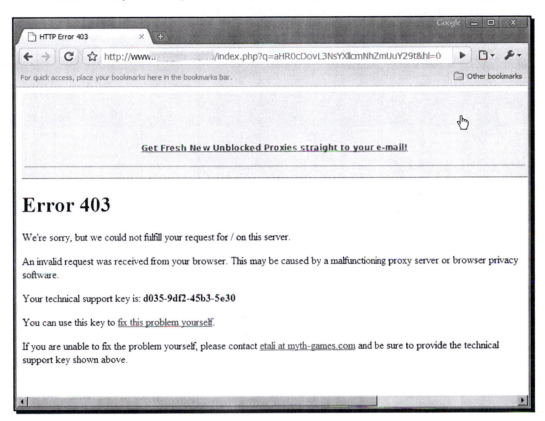

10. Blog owners can see requests that Bad Behavior has blocked under the **Tools | Bad Behavior** option in the **Site Admin** panel.

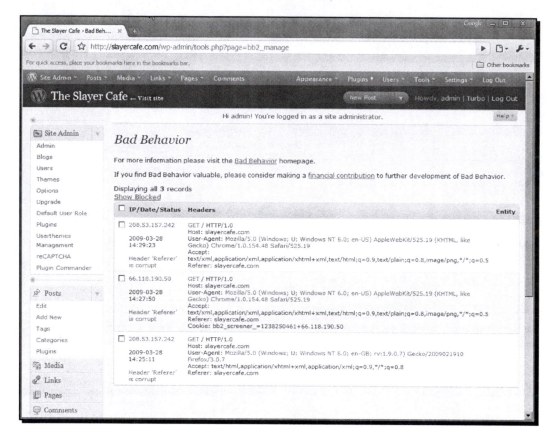

What just happened?

We have just set up the Bad Behavior plugin.

This plugin judges visitors using a range of criteria, including their **User Agent** (the browser that they claim they are using), their IP address, and the content of the request to make an educated guess as to the legitimacy of the request.

The plugin uses the blacklist known as http:BL from Project Honey Pot as an extra layer of protection. The blacklist contains a number of known spammer IP addresses.

Under the default settings, Bad Behavior will block bots that send requests, which do not look like those sent by a default browser. The http:BL will block known harvesters, spammers, and dictionary (or brute force) attackers.

One side effect of this system is that many users surfing via a proxy will be prevented from viewing your site, as shown in the screenshot below step eight. Whether this is acceptable to you will depend on how many of your normal users would be likely to use a proxy. If your site is aimed at Net Neutrality Campaigners, you may find that many of your users tend to surf using TOR, Your Freedom, or other similar proxy services out of habit or necessity based on the country in which they live. Rather than block those users, you may want to relax the rules used by Bad Behavior and use another spam protection service instead—perhaps one that analyzes the contents of the comment rather than the way the comment is being made.

SlayerCafe has chosen a strict approach to fighting spam. The site does have a few users who would need to surf via a proxy. It is quite common for Watchers to have to take a normal job in addition to their Watching. Typically, they work in libraries, book stores, and schools—places where web surfing is very controlled. Fortunately for us, Watchers are only a small percentage of our target audience and they are willing to accept the extra layer of security.

Fighting spam with Spam Karma and Akismet

There is not enough space in this chapter to cover all the spam-fighting solutions available for WordPress MU. A few others, however, do deserve a quick mention. Akismet is a very good spam-fighting solution, and one you may recognize if you have ever ran a normal WordPress blog. The multiuser version of Akismet usually costs money, although the developers are willing to consider offering their service for free to relatively low traffic, non-profit WordPress MU sites.

Spam Karma is a free spam fighting solution. The original developer ceased supporting the script in January 2009. He has released the source code under the GPL so that other developers can continue his work, so I would suggest you watch the WordPress forums to see if anyone picks up the project.

Have a go hero – taking spam prevention to the next level

If you feel you need more advanced spam protection, the Spam Karma project is worth a look. You can download the current source code from `http://code.google.com/p/spam-karma/`. It is a good idea to read the documentation and the issues page for the project before installing it, especially if you plan to run Spam Karma in conjunction with Bad Behavior.

If you would like to give back to the spam prevention community, take a look at Project Honey Pot. The project is looking for people to donate MX Records from domains that they do not use to receive email. They are also looking for people to run honey pots or to link to honey pots that others have set up.

If you have the server resources, or a spare domain to donate, take a look at the FAQ for Project Honey Pot at `http://www.projecthoneypot.org/faq.php`. If you don't have the resources, consider adding an invisible link to one of the honey pots in the footer of your site.

Making sure the plugins run for your users

In Chapter 3 we discussed the `mu-plugins` folder. WordPress MU plugins that are placed there will run automatically on your users' blogs. Unfortunately, some standard WordPress plugins do not behave in this manner.

To make sure that our users are protected by the spam-blocking plugins, we need to install a plugin manager that will automatically enable those plugins for each new blog when it is created.

Time for action – managing your users' plugins

There are two very good plugin management tools—Plugin Manager and Plugin Commander. Let's set them up.

1. Download Plugin Manager from `http://wpmudev.org/project/Plugin-Manager` and install it to the `wp-content/plugins` directory.

2. Do the same with Plugin Commander, which can be obtained from `http://firestats.cc/wiki/WPMUPluginCommander`.

3. Activate the two plugins in your **Site Admin** panel.

4. Go to **Site Admin | Plugins** and click on **Check Active Plugins**. You should see a list of the plugins your users currently have activated:

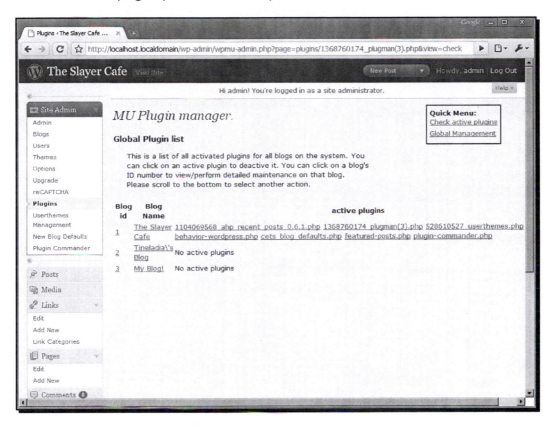

5. Under **Site Admin | Plugin Commander** you should see a list of all the plug-ins that you currently have installed on your blog:

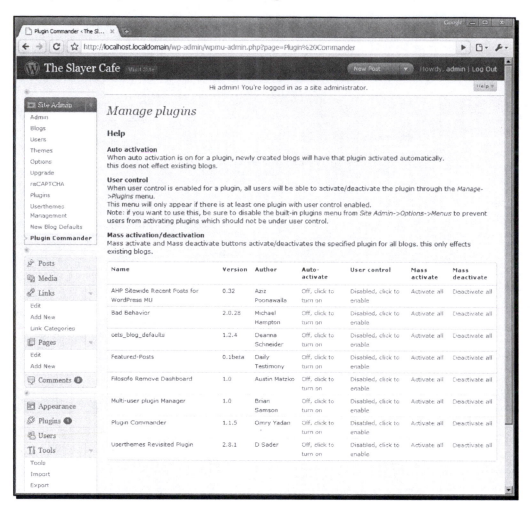

6. Click the **Auto-activate** link to turn on automatic activation of the plugins you would like to have active on all your users' blogs (for example, Bad Behavior and reCAPTCHA).

7. Click the **User control** link to enable user activation and deactivation of plugins that you would like to give your users the option to turn on and off— for example Featured-Posts and Sitewide Recent comments.

8. If you do not want your users to be able to turn off the plugins you have enabled for them, disable the Plugins menu via the **Site Admin | Options** page.

What just happened?

The two plugins that we have installed give us more control over the plugins that our users can have active.

Plugin Manager allows us to see which plugins our users have activated. This is useful because it allows us to make sure that very important plugins—such as anti-spam ones, are turned on for every blog. It will also be useful for tracking the use of plugins in the long term. Knowing which plugins are very popular and which ones are used by only a handful of people will help you figure out what your users like and the features they want to see on the site.

Plugin Commander can be used to force the activation of plugins. You can force all of your users (including existing ones) to activate or deactivate a plugin and you can use it to ensure that all new blogs come with certain plugins activated.

While some features such as the ability to embed videos in posts aren't essential, it is very important to ensure that spam protection measures are set up earlier for every blog. Your individual users may not mind if they get spam comments on their own blogs, but uncontrolled spam on one blog could adversely affect the way search engines view the entire site, which is bad for you and your site's other users.

Blocking bad guys with .htaccess

While the combination of a CAPTCHA and the suspicious behavior identification of Bad Behavior proves to be a very effective spam-prevention solution, spam is not the only problem that a webmaster has to worry about. There are several other issues such as bandwidth theft, email harvesters, and hackers.

The .htaccess file lets you give instructions to the server so that it knows how to handle each request. It's a very powerful file, but editing it can be slightly scary because a single typing error can prevent your entire site from loading.

Always back up your .htaccess file

The .htaccess file is one of the most important files on a web site. A single typographical error in that file can bring down your entire web site, and the errors that appear when your site is down may not make it obvious that the .htaccess file is the one causing the problem. Changes to the .htaccess file may also cause your site to behave in unusual ways, without immediately obvious error messages. To save yourself lots of troubleshooting time, always back up your .htaccess file, and be very careful when making changes to it!

Time for action – .htaccess settings to stop bad guys

1. Download your .htaccess file and make a copy of it called htaccess.txt—keep the original as a backup.

2. Open up htaccess.txt.

3. You should see a line that says RewriteEngine On near the top of the file. Read through the file to find where the lines beginning with RewriteCond or RewriteRule end.

4. After those lines, add the following:

```
RewriteCond %{HTTP_REFERER} !^$
RewriteCond %{HTTP_REFERER} !^http://(*.)?yourdomain.com/.*$ [NC]
RewriteRule .*\.(jpe?g|jpg|gif|bmp|png)$ http://www.
someimagehostingsite.domain/antihotlink.jpg
```

5. Also add the following lines:

```
RewriteCond  %{REQUEST_METHOD} HEAD
RewriteRule  .* - [F]
```

6. If you would like to block email harvesters, add the following:

```
RewriteCond %{HTTP_USER_AGENT} CherryPickerSE [OR]
RewriteCond %{HTTP_USER_AGENT} CherryPickerElite [OR]
RewriteCond %{HTTP_USER_AGENT} EmailCollector [OR]
RewriteCond %{HTTP_USER_AGENT} EmailSiphon [OR]
RewriteCond %{HTTP_USER_AGENT} EmailWolf [OR]
RewriteCond %{HTTP_USER_AGENT} ExtractorPro
RewriteRule .* [F,L]
```

7. If you would like to add some rules to stop spam bots and referrer spam, take a look at the .htaccess file created by AaronLogan.com (http://www.aaronlogan.com/downloads/htaccess.php)—the list of URLs and IP addresses is slightly old, but it is a good starting point.

8. Upload the file you have created and rename it back to .htaccess. Then check that everything on the site works as normal. If you experience problems, restore the old file while you double check the changes you made.

What just happened?

The `.htaccess` file tells the server how it should respond to requests for web pages.

In step three, we blocked image hotlinking. This stops people from being able to include an image hosted on our site in one of their web pages. The main reason for preventing people from doing this is that if an image hosted on our server gets posted to a popular site or, for that matter, several people take images and post them on less popular sites, that would cost us a lot of bandwidth.

Image hotlinking is a very bad etiquette. Some webmasters choose to redirect stolen images to a nasty or repulsive image with a message saying "Stop stealing bandwidth". Other options include simply serving up a 1x1 pixel gif, or telling the server to refuse the request. I recommend one of the latter approaches.

In step five we block HEAD requests, which are used by scanners that do not want to fetch the whole page. While there are a number of legitimate reasons for this, in most cases such applications are used by hackers wanting to scan for sites with certain vulnerabilities. They are also used by some denial of service tools. Blocking HEAD requests should not affect most legitimate visitors.

In the final two steps we blocked requests from suspicious user agents.

The User Agent is the name that a web browser, spam bot, or harvester sends to the server so that the server knows what it is talking to. Some programmers have made bots that can lie about their identity, but many bots do identify themselves correctly, so it is possible to ban them by name.

You may be wondering why you would want to use `.htaccess` files for this purpose when Bad Behavior already stops a lot of these attacks. Following are two main reasons:

- Firstly, an extra layer of protection is very useful. You may see some spam attacks or hacking attempts coming in from an address that Bad Behavior does not block. You can respond to this and update your `.htaccess` file to block the attacker as soon as you notice it, while you may have to wait a while for Bad Behavior to catch up.
- Secondly, the addresses you block in the `.htaccess` file won't even get to the stage of loading your site, which will mean that they take up less processor time, keeping the site nice and fast for legitimate visitors.

Have a go hero – build your own list

Now that you have an idea of what a .htaccess file could contain, why not try building your own list? If your web host offers AWStats, Webalizer, or any other stats tracking software, take a look at the logs. If you see something that doesn't look right, build a rule that will block it. Referrer spam, for example, is easy to spot—after all, why is an online pharmacy linking to a blog network for Vampire Slayers? I don't think they're selling treatments for neck wounds!

It's worth trying to keep your .htaccess file reasonably small. For example, rather than blocking lots of pharmacy sites individually, consider the following rule:

```
RewriteCond %{HTTP_REFERER} ^(http://)?(www\.)?.*(-|.)pharmacy(-|.).*$
[NC,OR]
```

Which would block all referrers that contain the word "pharmacy".

Be careful with blocking IP addresses or IP ranges. If that IP address is dynamically assigned, you may end up blocking a legitimate visitor by accident. If you find that you are getting a lot of spam or hacking attempts from a certain IP range, block it for a short time, but leave a comment (lines that are comments start with a #) noting why it is blocked along with the date; remove that block after a week or two and see if the attempts have stopped.

Once again, I would recommend you take a backup of your existing .htaccess file before making any changes to it.

Pop quiz – spam blocking

1. A spam blog is called a:
    a) Slog
    b) Spog
    c) Spag Bol (yum!)
    d) Splog

2. http:BL prevents spam by:
    a) Blocking all http requests because only spammers use http.
    b) Using your site as a honey pot to prevent spam.
    c) Reading the contents of new comments and blocking ones that contain links.
    d) Noting the IP address of the user and blocking it if it is on a blacklist of known spammers, hackers, and proxies.

3. `.htaccess` is:

   a) A method of accessing a server.

   b) A file containing configuration information for your Apache server, including how to respond to certain requests.

   c) A file containing lots of email addresses—used as a honey pot to bait spammers into giving themselves away.

   d) A Linux shell command that can be used to access a web site.

Answers: (1) d, (2) d, (3) b

More ways to secure your server

Server management is beyond the scope of this book. However, if you are running your own server or even a VPS, then learning about Apache security is a good idea. Some useful modules include `dosevasive`, `fail2ban`, and `mod_security`. You can read more about `mod_security` at `http://www.howtoforge.com/apache_mod_security`.

Other useful plugins

So far, we have added some plugins that will make the fight against spam easier. However, there's more to running a web site than stopping comment spammers, and fortunately there are plugins that can help us with virtually every aspect of running a site—from setting up the basic categories that new users will see on their blogs to moderating new user registrations, and even automating backups.

Moderating registrations

Slayercafe is intended for use by Slayers, Watchers, demon hunters, and their friends. The slaying community is a very tight-knit one, and it is likely that anyone who would want to join the site would either already know someone who is a member or would be able to somehow prove that they are involved in slaying related activities.

For SlayerCafe to remain a safe place for its members, it must be a closed community, with every single member approved by one of the Watchers responsible for maintaining the site. To do this, we can use the Moderate New Blogs plugin available at `http://wpmudev.org/project/Moderate-New-Blogs`. This plugin will ensure that new blogs require activation by a moderator. The Moderate New Blogs plugin does not prevent users from joining your community, but it does stop them from being able to use their blog until their account is activated.

Another useful plugin for regulating sign-ups is WP-Invites, which can be used to make your community invitate-only. This is ideal for sites that are still in beta phase and are not ready to accept members of the public. The plugin can be downloaded from `http://wpmudev.org/project/wp-invites`.

Taming your default categories

The default categories in WordPress MU are pretty boring, and they certainly don't cover the kind of things that Vampire Slayers would want to talk about. The chances are, they don't cover the subjects that are likely to be hot topics on your blog network either.

It is possible to change the default categories so that your users have some more interesting options for categorizing their posts. You can even update existing blogs using the "New blog default categories plus search and replace" plugin available at `http://wpmudev.org/project/new-blog-default-categories-plus-search-and-replace`.

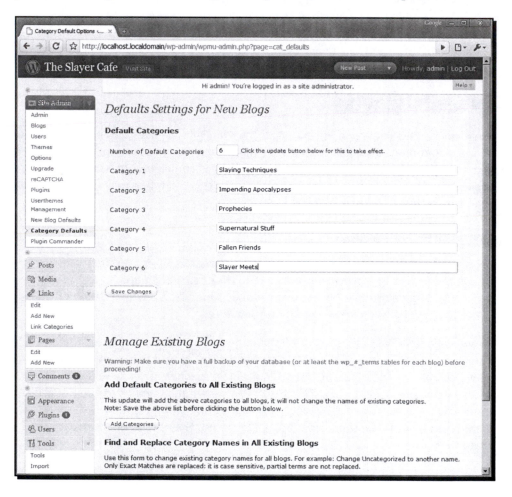

Using this plugin, you can set up default categories. SlayerCafe uses **Slaying Techniques**, **Impending Apocalypses**, **Prophecies**, and **Supernatural Stuff** as the default categories. You can also rename categories and have those changes reflected across all existing blogs. So, for example, if you were to decide that as almost all "Prophecies" are about "Impending Apocalypses", it is a waste to have two categories, and you could rename Prophecies to clarify that you meant longer term prophecies that had not been clearly interpreted yet.

Regular backups without lifting a finger

As your site grows, backups will become more and more important. If your server were to fail tomorrow, you would probably be rather annoyed at the thought of having to re-do all the work that you have done up to this point, but imagine how you would feel if it were to fail in a few months' time when you have a community of users who have built up profiles and blogs! Imagine having to tell those users that everything they have created has been lost!

Fortunately, you can automate most of the work of taking backups.

Time for action – automatic backups

1. Download PuTTY from
   `http://www.chiark.greenend.org.uk/~sgtatham/putty/`.

2. Log in to your web site's host using SSH and create a file called `dbsave`.

3. Paste in the following code replacing `wpdbuser` and `yourpassword` with your username and password, and `wordpress` with the name of your database.

   ```
   #! /bin/sh
   DATE=`date | tr " " _`
   echo $DATE
   mysqldump wordpress --add-drop-table -h localhost -u wpdbuser -p
   yourpassword | gzip > db.$DATE.gz
   tar cvfz code.$DATE.gz
   ```

4. Save the file. Then at the command prompt type `sh dbsave`. The script should create a `.gz` file containing a backup of your database.

5. At the command prompt, type `crontab -e`.

6. At the end of the file, enter something like this:

   ```
   0       0       1,15,29       0       0 sh dbsave
   ```

Cron Jobs and Crontab

Are you curious about that row of numbers? If you'd like to learn more about how to schedule jobs to run automatically, read up on the Unix command Crontab at `http://www.adminschoice.com/docs/crontab.htm`.

Cron jobs are used to schedule a job to run every X period of time. You can select minutes or hours, or you can have a job run on a certain day of the month, a certain month, or a certain day of the week. The numbers in the command we used above set the schedule, while `sh dbsave` is the command we want to run—in our case, a shell script that exports the database to a `.gz` file.

What just happened?

We have used a simple shell script to create a backup of our WordPress MU database, and we have created a cron job that will run the script every 14 days.

The script saves the backup to our server. This will not protect us if the server itself goes down. It is a good idea to have a current backup of the database stored somewhere other than your own web server. You could use a free FTP application that supports scheduled transfers (such as `http://www.primasoft.com/ftp.htm`) to set up a regular automated download of the database backup.

You could also tweak the script to email the database backup using the following command:

```
mutt -a code.$DATE.gz -s "Database Backup" your@emailaddress.com </
dev/null
```

Mutt is a popular email program, and the above line of code will tell Mutt to send an email to your email address with the subject "Database Backup" and an attachment containing the latest backup.

I use a Gmail account for this purpose and leave the mail on the server. That way, in the unlikely event of the SlayerCafe server going down the same time my house gets raided by vampires, there is still a backup stored somewhere else for the other Watchers to use to restore the site.

Don't forget to take backups of the files that make up your WordPress MU install, too. The themes and PHP files won't change anywhere near as often as the database, but they are still important to back up.

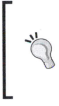

Logging in to your server via SSH

If you aren't sure what your SSH login details are, check the email your host sent you when you signed up. In most cases, the SSH login details are the same as your cPanel details. If you can't use SSH, don't worry—look for a Cron manager in your control panel and see if you can set up the job in there.

Have a go hero – other ways to do backups

There are a number of plugins for normal WordPress that automate backups. If you are not able to run cron jobs on your server or if you do not have shell access, you should try one of those. However, before you rely on such a plugin, you should verify that the backup is working properly. The plugins usually will not have been tested with WordPress MU, so depending on how they are coded, you may find that certain tables may be omitted from the backup. It is best to find that out early, rather than think your files are safe only to find out in an emergency that there are parts missing!

If you have cPanel hosting, check out the backup features that it offers. You may find it convenient to use cPanel's backup features to do a full file and database backup, and then transfer the backup to an off-site host via FTP or email it to an email account with a lot of storage space.

Summary

In this chapter we have covered a number of ways to secure our blog, as well as ways to automate backups.

We talked about stopping spammers by using Bad Behavior and http:BL to stop bots from being able to comment and by using reCAPTCHA to confirm that any comments submitted were made by a human being.

We also talked about protecting your site from spammers and hackers using .htaccess file settings.

Protecting your site from hackers is vital, but hacking isn't the only threat to your site. To help protect yourself from data loss—either due to server failure or just a failed WordPress MU upgrade—we learned about automating database backups and emailing them to yourself so that you have a copy of the backup that is not stored on the same server as the site itself.

Finally, we looked at some ways to control who joins the site and learned how to manage the plugins that are active on your users' blogs.

We also discussed the ways in which you can help in the fight against spam beyond just protecting your own blogs, and looked at some other useful plugins that can help you manage your site, including making your site invitate-only and managing the blog categories available to your users by default.

Now that your site is a safe and spam free environment, it's time to bring in some users to liven the place up. In the next chapter we will look at ways to increase traffic and bring in users so that your blog network can become a thriving community.

6

Increasing Traffic to Your Blog

In the previous chapter we looked at ways to keep our blog network spam free and safe for our blog authors and their readers. Now that we've done this, we need to spread the word about the blog network to make sure that as many slayers as possible start using the site. This chapter will look at some popular traffic and visitor retention enhancing features of WordPress MU such as tagging, pings, trackbacks, and RSS.

In this chapter we will look at:

- ◆ Allowing your visitors to use tags to categorize their posts
- ◆ Advertising blog updates with pings
- ◆ Sending trackbacks when you post about other blogs
- ◆ Letting visitors subscribe to blogs via RSS feeds
- ◆ Advertising blog updates on Twitter

So let's get started...

Improved tagging

Tags are a way to label content to make it easier to find later. Tags are a complement to the traditional "categories" way of organizing things. Blog owners can label a post with tags that describe the important content, making it easier for visitors and search engines to find those posts at a later date. You can add as many tags as you wish to a post, giving you extra freedom to tag subjects even if you don't think you'll be posting on that topic regularly. In this way, tags are less restrictive than categories.

As an example, one of our Slayers may write a blog post on the Impending Apocalypse of 2009, where stuffed toys come to life and attempt to kill their owners. If this apocalypse was quickly averted, they may write only one blog post about it, which would be posted under the "Impending Apocalypses" category. There's no point making an entire new category for strange happenings surrounding stuffed toys, as it's unlikely to be a subject that would see many posts, but tagging the post with "apocalypse" and "stuffed toys" would help if any future Slayers encountered killer teddy bears at some point in the future.

Time for action – tagging blog posts

WordPress MU does have a simple, built-in form of **tagging** system, but it isn't very convenient to use, and many users may decide it's too much trouble to add new tags and figure out which tags to mark each blog post with. Let's offer them a more convenient and nicer looking way of doing things.

1. Download WP Auto Tagger from
   `http://wordpress.org/extend/plugins/wp-auto-tagger/`.

2. Upload the contents of the ZIP file to your `/wp-content/plugins` directory.

3. Enable the WP-Auto Tagger Plugin on your main blog via the **Site Admin** panel.

4. Try creating a new post on the main blog. Beside the main post entry box you should see some new tag tools.

5. Clicking on the **Suggest Tags** button should give you a list of appropriate tags.

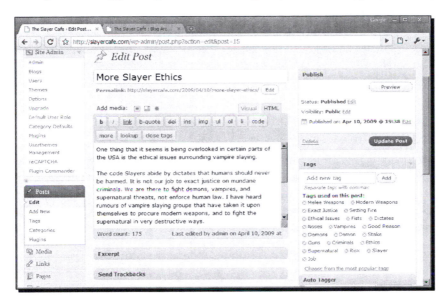

6. Submit the post and then look at the main blog. You should see some tags on the front page and tags on your new post, too.

7. Using Plugin Commander, enable the plugin for your users.

Suggest tags not working?

If you get the **curl not enabled** message when you click on suggest tags or you simply see no suggested tags appear, you will need to have your web host enable curl for you. Some web hosts disable lib-curl by default because of security concerns, but most are willing to enable it if requested to do so.

What just happened?

We have set up an improved tagging system that our users may find very useful. The plugin will read new blog posts and suggest tags for them, saving our users the hassle of typing out tags for each post. Of course, our users can choose to type out the tags by hand if they prefer and can delete any tags that the plugin suggests if they don't like them; however, they should find that they get some very useful inspiration from the suggest tags feature.

SlayerCafe displays a list of tags on the right-hand side of the blog. Tags that appear frequently show in a bigger font than tags that are used less often. This gives visitors an overview of the main focus of each blog.

Sitewide tags

Now that you have tags displaying for each individual user blog, let's offer a page with a tag cloud, which includes tags from all the blogs on the site.

Time for action – sitewide tag clouds

1. Download the WordPress MU Sitewide Tags application from

   http://wordpress.org/extend/plugins/wordpress-mu-sitewide-tags/.

2. Upload the plugin to your /wp-content/plugins folder.

3. Enable the plugin via the **Site Admin** panel.

4. Go to **Site Options**, scroll down to the bottom of the page, and check the **Tags Blog** box to enable tags.

5. Check the **Tags can be indexed by Search Engines** box.

6. Make a post or two on your test blogs, and then visit the tags subdomain for your site; you should see something like this:

What just happened?

We have just set up an improved tagging system for our users. The WP Auto Tagger plugin pulls out words that it thinks are important from blog posts and uses them as tags. The plugin isn't perfect and it does sometimes come up with silly suggestions, but users can remove tags that they don't want, or replace them with their own.

The Auto Tagger plugin ensures that even users who don't take the time to pick out their own tags will still have the option of having some kind of tagging system.

Why is this important? Well, think ahead to this time next year—imagine how many posts the average user will have on their blog. Now imagine trying to find those posts by category. Athena may have made a post on SlayerCafe about the apocalypse that Watcherlicious almost caused when she read the wrong spell from the Dark Magikus book, but finding that post in the category "Impending Apocalypses" would be a time-consuming task when you consider that Athena fights to stop an apocalypse almost every week!

If Athena used a tagging system, then it is likely that this particular apocalypse related post would have been tagged with "Watcherlicious" and with "Dark Magikus", making it much easier to find.

We also set up a sitewide tagging system. This adds a stream of all new posts to a central blog. Watchers can keep an eye on this blog to see what's happening on a broader level, that is, *what are people talking about* and *what are the most important issues*.

The most commonly appearing tags appear in a bolder, bigger font. You can see that at the moment our biggest theme is Slayers. Obviously, there's not much exciting happening on the vampire slaying front at the moment, as the Slayers are just talking amongst themselves about general slayer stuff. If the theme of conversation suddenly changed to "demonic robots", then that tag would appear prominently and the Watchers would know very quickly that there is a global demonic robot problem.

The sitewide tags page is useful from a search engine perspective too, as it presents the most recent content to the search engines in one convenient place.

Have a go hero – styling the tags page

Our tags page at the moment looks just like a normal blog and has a rather boring name—`tags.slayercafe.com`.

You can rename the tags page in the **Site Options** panel on the main blog. A better name might be "pulse" or "live-stream".

The default setting indexes the last 5000 posts. This number can be changed, but don't set it too high as it could tax the server.

Try customizing the layout of the Tags blog. The blog network's admin account can be used to log into the Tags blog's admin panel so that you can change the theme and make some other tweaks such as adding widgets.

If you want to take things a step further, take a look at `http://www.wordpress.com/tags`. Here you can see a great example of a streamlined "what's hot on our network" tags page.

You may have noticed that the **Tags** blog appears under **Recent User Posts**, so new posts appear twice—once by the original poster and once under **Tags**. Check the blog ID number of the Tags blog, and try changing the code we created earlier so that the posts to the Tags blog don't display.

Using pings

WordPress MU is set up to **ping** a service called **Ping-o-Matic** when new posts are made. This service is useful for English language blogs and for bloggers in America in particular because most of the services that Ping-o-Matic works with are U.S. centric. But there are other services that may be more suitable for bloggers in other countries or even blogs in specific niches. Let's look at ways to add extra ping services to our list of sites to ping for each blog.

Time for action – pings

1. Open up `/wp-admin/includes/schema.php`.

2. Find the line that says

    ```
    add_option('ping_sites', 'http://rpc.pingomatic.com/');
    ```

3. Change that line so that it reads

    ```
    add_option('ping_sites', "http://rpc.pingomatic.com/\nhttp://
                                    rpc.NEWPINGSITE.TLD");
    ```

4. You can add multiple sites as long as you separate each URL with a \n.

5. Save and upload the file.

6. Any future blogs will be created with the new ping sites set in **Site Options**.

7. You can update existing sites either via MySQL or by using the **Site Admin** panel.

What just happened?

We have added a few extra sites to the list of ping services that will be notified when a new post is made.

A ping is an example of a push mechanism. Instead of **blog aggregation services** having to look at all the blogs, they are listed to see which ones have new content. The blogs themselves inform the aggregators that they have been updated by sending them a ping.

Ping-o-Matic is a service that receives pings and then passes them on to multiple servers. This reduces the amount of servers you have to ping, saving you time when you publish an article. However, Ping-o-Matic may not cover every site you would want to ping.

We have added only two sites to the ping list—WhiteWiccaBlogs and TheWatcherNetwork. We don't want to draw too much attention from normal people on sites such as NewsNow or the My Yahoo service.

Try to keep the number of individual sites you ping to a minimum. Not only is there a possibility that pinging huge numbers of sites could make adding posts take longer, pinging sites that are outside the topic of your blog is unlikely to get you any valuable traffic. It is better to focus on gaining visits from people who are actually interested in your blog network's subject.

For an English language blog, using Ping-o-Matic, Technorati, and Google would be a good start. If your network is aimed at people who speak a different language, pinging local news aggregators would be a good idea.

Have a go hero – more sites to ping

Take a look at the list of sites in the following table, and think about the type of blog you have and the people you want to reach. The sites in the table are very general ones. You may find that there are aggregator services out there for your niche—be that houses in Singapore, computer games, or travel. A Google search for "keyword aggregator" should help you find the right kind of sites.

Once you've chosen the sites you would like to ping, remember that each URL is separated by the characters \n and you need to surround the entire list in double quotes (" "), not single ones (' ').

Site	URL
FeedBurner	http://ping.feedburner.com
My Yahoo	http://api.my.yahoo.com/rss/ping
Syndic8	http://ping.syndic8.com/xmlrpc.php
Myblog.jp (Japanese)	http://ping.bloggers.jp/rpc/
Newsgator	http://rpc.newsgator.com/
Blogg.de (German)	http://xmlrpc.blogg.de/
Blogshares.com	http://www.blogshares.com/rpc.php

Blogshares.com is a fun site. It is a fantasy blog share market, where your blog is valued depending on the number of incoming links it has. Depending on your blog network's niche, it may not be a great source of targeted traffic, but it is certainly fun to play with.

Trackbacks

Trackbacks are another popular blogging tool. A trackback is often used instead of a comment. A reader who owns their own blog may write something about a post they have seen on your blog network and send a trackback to the relevant blog owner using the trackback link. The trackback then appears as a comment with a link back to the post the reader wrote on their blog. Trackbacks look just like normal comments, except the text contains a short excerpt from the blog post that the trackback was sent from:

> **1 RESPONSE SO FAR ↓**
>
> **So, will SlayerCafe be getting an upgrade? « My Life** //
> September 10, 2009 at 8:31 am | Reply (edit)
>
> [...] will SlayerCafe be getting an upgrade? By etali WordPress-MU 2.7.1 has
> been released – does that mean that SlayerCafe will be getting an upgrade? I
> can't [...]

WordPress MU supports trackbacks by default; blog owners can send a trackback by pasting the correct trackback link into the **Send Trackbacks** box on the **Write Post** page. Trackbacks can be sent at the time of posting or by using a cron job that sends all pending trackbacks in one go.

To accept trackbacks, you will need to make sure that the option **Allow link notifications from other blogs** is ticked on the **Discussion Settings** page.

Offering RSS feeds

You may have seen the **RSS** icon on some web sites. It's usually orange and has three little "signal waves" on it. This icon is pretty globally recognized now, and many people subscribe to RSS feeds via their Google or Yahoo accounts without realizing that it is the RSS they are using.

WordPress MU offers some RSS links for comments and new posts via the Meta widget, but those are just text links. Let's offer a clearer way for users to subscribe to blogs on your blog network.

Time for action – offering RSS subscription options

1. Download the Add to Any Subscribe plugin from
    `http://wordpress.org/extend/plugins/add-to-any/`.

2. Upload the `plugin` folder to `/wp-content/plugins`.

3. Activate the plugin sitewide.

4. Go to **Settings | Share/Save Buttons**; you should see a screen like this:

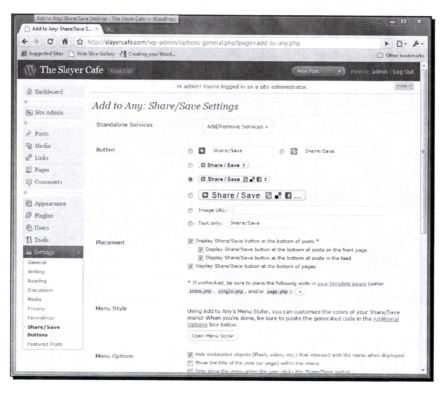

5. Select the size of the subscribe button you would like.

6. Untick **Display Share/Save button** at the bottom of pages.

7. If you are not fond of menus that expand when you roll over them, you may want to select **Only show the menu when the user clicks the subscribe button**.

8. Leave **Hide embedded objects...** checked. This stops any videos from interfering with the menu when it pops out.

9. Save your changes and add the widget to your sidebar. You can click and drag on the blue widget bars to move the **Add to Any** widget to the top. Your menu should look something like this:

10. If visitors click on the Share/Save icon, they will be taken to a page with the full list of bookmarking options, which looks something like the following (the list scrolls, so not all bookmarking options are visible in the screenshot):

FeedBurner

FeedBurner can be used to track the number of RSS feed subscribers you have and how many of those subscribers are actively engaged with your feed. Setting up FeedBurner is quite simple, although you will need to register for an account at `http://feedburner.google.com`. If you already have an account at the old `Feedburner.com` site, you can move the feeds to your Google account when you sign in.

Time for action – let's burn some feeds

1. Download the Feedburner FeedSmith plugin from `http://feedburner.google.com/fb/static/feedburner_feedsmith_plugin_2.3.zip`.

2. Upload the plugin's PHP file to `/wp-content/plugins`.

3. Activate the plugin for yourself, then for all other users.

4. Log in to `Feedburner.google.com` and add your site's feed to your FeedBurner account by entering the URL into the **Burn a feed right this instant** box.

5. In most cases the default title and address should be fine; you may want to change the address if yours is too cumbersome. For `Slayercafe.com`, FeedBurner picked `http://feeds2.feedburner.com/TheSlayerCafe`, which is nice and easy to remember.

6. On the next screen, tick the box to allow FeedBurner to track Clickthroughs and Reach.

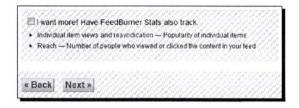

7. Go to the **Publicize** tab and activate the FeedCount feature.

8. On your main blog, go to the **Settings | FeedBurner** screen and paste the URL you created in step 5 into the FeedBurner box.

9. Install the FeedBurner Widget available at
`http://wordpress.org/extend/plugins/feedburner-widget/`.

10. On the **Appearance | Widgets** page, add the widget just above the normal RSS feed, and set it up like shown in the following screenshot. You should now have two subscription options on your front page.

11. Once your site starts getting subscribers, you should see some useful statistics on the FeedBurner Analyze page.

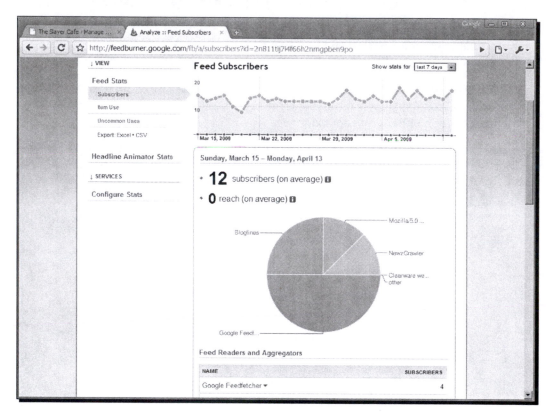

What's my feed URL?

If you aren't sure what your feed's URL is, check out the following list:

- ◆ RSS 2.0: `http://www.mydomain.tld/feed/`
- ◆ RSS 2.0: `http://www.mydomain.tld/feed/rss2/`
- ◆ RSS 0.92: `http://www.mydomain.tld/feed/rss/`
- ◆ RDF/RSS 1.0: `http://www.mydomain.tld/feed/rdf/`
- ◆ Atom: `http://www.mydomain.tld/feed/atom/`

All of the above feed types are offered by WordPress MU. The RSS 2.0 feed will be the one that is most frequently asked for by directories and aggregators; however, it is useful to know the address of the other feeds in case a site requests them.

What just happened?

We have just set up two different ways for people to subscribe to the main blog, and we have offered our blog network's users the chance to do the same with their blogs. Our users will need to create their own FeedBurner accounts, but the rest of the work has been done for them—they just need to add the right widgets to their page.

Offering two different ways to subscribe may seem strange, especially when you consider that the count shown by FeedBurner is inaccurate because it doesn't track people who subscribed using the direct link.

The reason I have chosen to do it this way is because FeedBurner offers some useful statistics, such as how many people clicked through and which readers they are using, about the users that have subscribed via its feeds. If you find that you have a huge number of subscribers but they are never clicking on articles, then perhaps your headlines aren't enticing enough. FeedBurner also tracks Uncommon Uses—for example, someone scraping your feed to use as free content for a spam blog.

If FeedBurner is so useful, then why offer an alternative? Well, not all RSS readers can understand FeedBurner feeds. This is especially true if your site expects a lot of visitors from people using older mobile devices. Offering a plain old RSS feed option is a good idea; otherwise, you will lose those subscribers entirely.

Remember that if FeedBurner ever goes down, your FeedBurner subscribers will not be able to read your RSS feed. In my experience as a subscriber, FeedBurner is a reliable service; as you would expect because the service is now owned by Google, and I feel that the usefulness of the statistics it offers outweighs the risk of downtime. You may feel differently about using a third-party service to manage your feeds. If you cannot afford any downtime, then perhaps serving your feeds directly is a better option.

Have a go hero – offering more RSS options

If you think that the Add to Any button is too intrusive, or if you want to offer subscribe links in more than one place (for example, as a widget in the sidebar and also as a link at the bottom of a post), then you can use the following text link code to add the different kinds of feed links.

Link	Format
`<?php bloginfo('rss2_url'); ?>`	RSS 2.0
`<?php bloginfo('rss_url'); ?>`	RSS 0.92
`<?php bloginfo('rdf_url'); ?>`	RSS 1.0
`<?php bloginfo('atom_url'); ?>`	Atom
`<?php bloginfo('comments_rss2_url'); ?>`	RSS Feed For Comments

You can use the code presented in this table anywhere you would like to have the RSS icons appear. Personally, I like to display the RSS icons in a prominent position in the right sidebar by editing `r_sidebar.php`.

Twitter and social bookmarking

People love to share information about cool sites they have found and interesting posts they have read. Taking advantage of this is a great way to bring in extra traffic. If you make it easy for visitors to your blog network to share the things they see and easy for your bloggers to promote the things they are doing, then you should get a decent amount of "free" promotion—assuming the content on your site is worthwhile, of course.

Twitter is a **microblogging** service that is enjoying a huge amount of success at the moment. It allows you to share the answer to the question "what are you doing?", as long as your answer is 140 characters or less! If you aren't already a member of Twitter, why not join? It's free to make an account on `www.twitter.com`, and even the busiest people in the world should have time to share the occasional 140 character message!

One common answer to that question is "posting a new blog entry" with a convenient link so that others can read it.

The Twitter Tools plugin allows you to send **Tweets** (the name for a message on Twitter) from your blog and will also post a Tweet every time you make a new blog post. The plugin will be very popular with users of your blog network who have a Twitter account. The plugin is available at `http://wordpress.org/extend/plugins/twitter-tools/`.

Getting your readers to share posts

Social bookmarking sites such as Digg, Reddit, Furl, and Del.icio.us, can be good sources of traffic if your bloggers write about topics within the niches covered by those sites.

Submitting to those sites can be time consuming, but you can make it easier for readers to submit posts they like by showing them a simple "Submit" button at the bottom of each post.

Time for action – social bookmarking links

1. Download the social bookmarking script from
`http://lesleyharrison.wordpress.org`.

2. Upload the `/images/` folder to the root of your web site.

3. Upload the `social-bookmarking.js` file to the root of your site.

4. Open the `index.php` file of the theme you are using on the main blog and look
for the line that says:

```
<p><?php _e('Sorry, no posts matched your criteria.');
                ?></p><?php endif; ?><br />
```

5. Add the following code after this line:

```
<h1>Bookmark This</h1>
<style="text-align: center;"><script src="http://www.slayercafe.
               com/social-bookmarking.js"></script>
```

6. Do the same for any themes that are likely to be used by your users.

7. When you view a post, you should see some bookmarking buttons at the bottom.

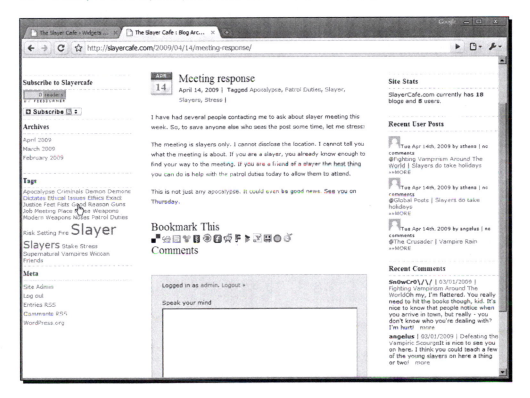

What just happened?

We have added a simple JavaScript bookmarking script to all of the sites on our blog. The script is created by Hugo Haas (http://larve.net/people/hugo/) and is easy to edit and maintain.

If you don't like the services that are listed, you can remove them by looking for the line that references them—for example, to remove Segnalo just delete the line that says the following:

```
add_tool('segnalo', 'Segnalo', 'http://segnalo.com/post.html.php?url='
+ url + '&amp;title=' + title);
```

To add a new bookmarking tool, you will need to find out the URL format that it uses for submissions and then add a line to the script that reads as follows:

```
add_tool('SITENAME', 'SITENAME', 'http://SITEURL/SUBMISSIONURL.
php?url=' + url + '&amp;title=' + title);
```

Then, create an image in the /images/ folder called SITENAME.png.

Have a go hero – Digg this

If you are running a site such as a technology, gaming, or programming-related blog network that would attract Digg readers, then you could add a Digg button to each new post that shows the number of "Diggs" the post has had and allows the reader to submit the post to Digg.com if it has not already been submitted.

Here is the code for such a button:

```
<script src="http://digg.com/tools/diggthis.js" type="text/
javascript"></script>
```

You don't have to limit yourself to Digg; there is a huge range of social bookmarking sites to choose from. Not all of those sites will suit your niche, but the ones that do could be a great source of traffic.

For some inspiration, refer to the list of popular social bookmarking web sites available at http://www.searchenginejournal.com/125-social-bookmarking-sites-importance-of-user-generated-tags-votes-and-links/6066/.

Pop quiz – traffic building

1. Trackbacks are:

   a) Sent to blog aggregators when a new post is made.

   b) Sent by blog owners when they write a blog post that links to yours.

   c) A way to undo a blog post you have made by mistake.

2. Pings, in the context of the blog world, are:

   a) A way you can check if a server is accepting connections.

   b) Sent out from your blog to inform blog aggregators a new post has been made.

   c) A noise made when a visitor clicks on a link on your blog.

3. FeedBurner can be used to:

   a) Keep track of how many people have subscribed to your blog.

   b) Alert you if your blog's feed is being used for unusual purposes.

   c) All of the above.

   Answers: (1) b, (2) b, (3) c

More about traffic building

The above are just a few useful traffic-building tools. There are many other ways you can increase your traffic and track your visitors' statistics. One thing you should look at is **Google Analytics** (http://analytics.google.com), which is a free and very detailed traffic statistics application that lets you see where visitors are coming from, how long they stay on your site, and what they do while they are there.

Google also offers a number of other helpful webmaster tools, including ones that will flag errors on your site and help you diagnose problems that may be affecting your search engine ranking.

Summary

This chapter touched on some ways you can increase traffic to your blog.

We learned how to use pings to send updates to blog aggregators so that they know that there is new content on your site. We also learned how to use the trackback feature so that bloggers can have a dialogue with each other and can carry out a discussion via blog posts and comments.

We learned about tagging—allowing users to tag their posts, making it easier to find posts about a certain topic at a later date. We looked at the benefits of RSS feeds, both for allowing content syndication and for letting users subscribe to individual blogs so that they know when new posts have been made.

Social bookmarking sites were discussed as well. We learned how to add a **Bookmark This** button to our blog posts, which should encourage our readers to share the post with their friends and fellow social bookmarking site users.

We also looked tracking statistics about the usage your RSS feeds, along with sending updates to Twitter by offering a sitewide tags page so that visitors can get an overview of what the community as a whole is talking about.

Now that we've covered the most popular traffic-building features, let's take a look at some ways to keep your visitors once they arrive. The next chapter will look at sticky features, such as polls and gravatars, that engage your blog network's visitors and make them feel like they are part of the community.

7
Sticky Features for your Blog Network

One trap that many web site owners fall into is spending lots of time pulling in traffic but not offering anything to encourage visitors to return. This leads to a rather self-defeating cycle where the site owner is forced to constantly promote their site to keep bringing in the same number of visitors, eating up valuable time that could be spent improving the site in other ways.

Fortunately, a little time invested during the early days of building a site can pay off very well in terms of encouraging repeat visitors.

In this chapter we will:

- Learn what is meant by making a site "sticky"
- Look at ways to build conversations with visitors through comments and contact forms
- Make our visitors feel like they are part of a community with gravatars, polls, and welcome messages
- Find out how to encourage visitors to subscribe to the site, and keep them coming back

So let's get started...

What do people mean by "sticky"?

If you have ever ran a blog or web site before, you may have noticed that it's fairly easy to get a spike in traffic by submitting a good story to a few social bookmarking sites or by being lucky enough to get a link to one of your posts from a much larger site.

The problem is that after a day or so, when the submissions fall off the front page, it's likely your traffic will die down to its usual levels again. Some site owners fall into the trap of chasing after the next traffic spike, using "linkbait" articles with intentionally controversial titles and content, when they should really be focusing on quality content, improving the site, and working towards sustained growth.

Many bloggers submit their site to `StumbleUpon.com`. StumbleUpon is a web service where users can enter their interests, and be sent to a random site that will match those interests. Those users can then either give a "thumbs up" to the site they are sent to indicating that they like the site or a "thumbs down" if they don't like it. Those votes are used to improve future suggestions and increase the chances of the next site that they "Stumble Upon" being one that they are interested in.

Other popular sites for increasing traffic include Technorati (a site that measures the "authority" of a blog based on how many other bloggers are linking to it), and the news/story-related sites Reddit (a general interest site with everything from politics to gadgets-related news), and Digg (a site with a focus on tech and gaming news).

A sticky blog is one that doesn't just attract new visitors, it keeps them. Instead of having a visitor click through from a link on Technorati or visit by using the Stumble! feature of StumbleUpon, skim the page they land on and then leave, a sticky blog would make that visitor stay around a little longer.

Ideally, visitors would read the article they were interested in and then find themselves intrigued enough to read more articles. They may comment on some articles and then keep returning to read answers to their comments. Or, they may decide to subscribe to the blog so that they can read future posts.

A sticky site encourages readers to become engaged with the community, resulting in long-term increases in traffic. When new readers arrive at the site for the first time, they get involved themselves and keep coming back. They may also tell their friends or link to the site from their own sites, giving you free promotion.

Letting readers and authors communicate

Interesting content is vital, but one of the best ways to get people coming back to your blog network is to give them a chance to interact with the site's authors and with each other. This not only makes the readers feel valued, it also opens up a dialogue that encourages repeat visitors.

Contact forms

Providing visitors with a way to contact you privately is useful for several reasons. The visitor may want to discuss advertising opportunities, submit some news you may be interested in, or ask for help with a problem they have accessing part of the site.

You could post your email address on the site, but this makes you vulnerable to spam attacks. A contact form is a safer way to allow your visitors to contact you.

Time for action – setting up contact forms

Let's set up a contact form:

1. Download Contact Form 7 from
   `http://wordpress.org/extend/plugins/contact-form-7/`.

2. To install, upload the contents of the archive file to `/wp-content/plugins`.

3. Activate the plugin and go to the settings page (**Tools | Contact Form 7**). You can also access the page by clicking **Settings** under the plugin name, which appears on the **Manage Plugins** page.

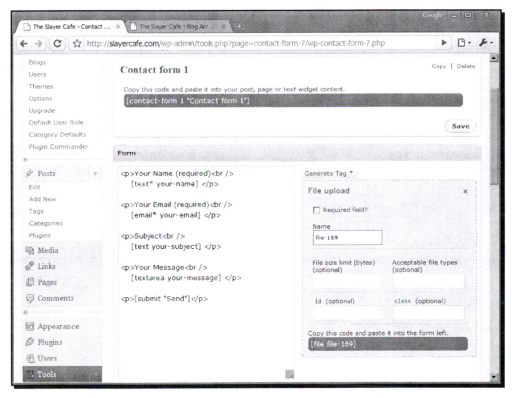

4. You can add new fields using the **Generate Tag** drop-down menu.

5. Further down the admin page you will see options to set error messages (such as the message users will see if they miss out a required field, or if they try to upload a file that is too big).

6. Once you have created the form, make a note of the tag at the top of the screen (in our case this was `[contact-form 1 "Contact form 1"]`).

7. Create a new page (**Pages | Add New**) called **Contact Us**, add a short message to the page, and then paste the contact form tag into the page.

8. Depending on the theme you are using, you may need to add the **Pages** widget to your sidebar so that visitors can find the new page.

9. Your page should look something like this:

What just happened?

Contact Form 7 is a powerful contact form tool that supports CAPTCHAs (via the Really Simple CAPTCHA plugin), file uploads, drop-down menus, and more.

You can define multiple contact forms and have each one submit to a different email address. This could be useful if you wish to have different people contacted for, say, advertising queries, news submissions, and tech support.

You can also have a contact form submit to multiple email addresses. So, as well as having the relevant person receive a copy of each message, the site administrator could ensure they receive a copy of all messages too.

You can set a prefix for each message, in addition to the subject line the visitor sets. For example, if you set the prefix to [Slayer-Form1], all emails from that contact form will have a subject line that begins with that text. You can use this to set up filters in your email application, making it easy to prioritize emails from different contact forms.

Improved comments

The basic WordPress MU comment feature allows readers to post their thoughts about a blog post, but it is not very good for encouraging discussion. One useful service for bloggers is **IntenseDebate**. This service allows for threaded discussion in comments, subscription to comments by RSS and email, and the ability to tie blog commenting in with other social networking sites and follow comments made by other blog readers.

Time for action – IntenseDebate Comments

1. Download the IntenseDebate Comments plugin from
   `http://wordpress.org/extend/plugins/intensedebate/`.

2. You will need to sign up for an account at `http://intensedebate.com/`.

3. Activate the plugin.

4. Go to **Settings | IntenseDebate**. You will be presented with a login screen. Enter the account details for the account you created in step 2.

5. Once you have logged in, click **Start Importing Comments**.

6. The import process can take a very long time, even if you don't have many comments to import.

7. Once the import process is complete, you can tweak the settings to suit your blog—although I found the default ones were a good starting point.

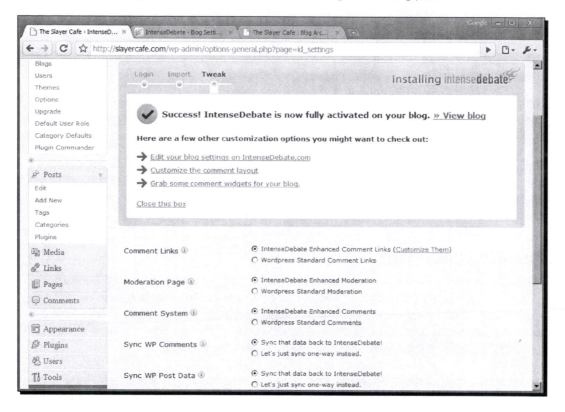

8. The IntenseDebate Comments plugin has its own **Comments** caption, so you may want to remove the Comments header from the `index.php` file in your theme folder.

9. The new comment box should look something like this:

10. You can moderate comments using the already familiar WordPress MU interface or the dashboard on the IntenseDebate site.

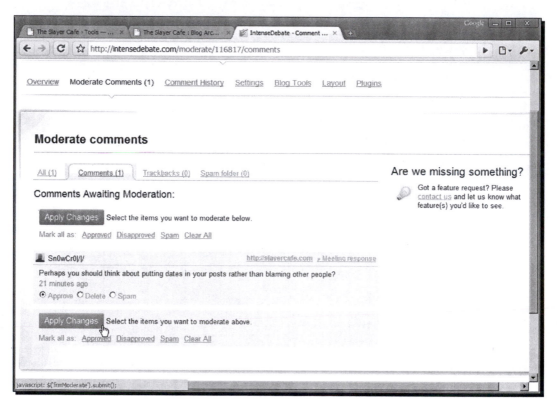

What just happened?

IntenseDebate is a commenting system that sits on top of WordPress and WordPress MU. It is ideal for all blogs, whether they are part of a blog network, or a standalone blog. It does not replace the existing WordPress comment system; it only complements it. This means you can use IntenseDebate in conjunction with other plugins that rely on the WordPress MU comment system.

Readers can comment on your blog using the IntenseDebate comment system. If they have JavaScript turned off, they will be presented with the normal WordPress comment system instead.

IntenseDebate has lots of useful features that will make your users feel a greater sense of engagement with your site's authors. Those features are described below:

◆ **Threaded discussions**:

IntenseDebate supports threaded comments. This makes it easy for readers to follow the discussions going on in the comments section. Readers can reply to the blog post itself, or reply to a specific comment, and IntenseDebate will break related comments into threads so that the discussion is easy to keep track of.

◆ **Track comments or comment anonymously**:

Readers can comment anonymously, or, if they have an IntenseDebate profile they can log in to it and comment using it. Any comments made will be stored in the WordPress comments database and also be sent to IntenseDebate.

◆ **Subscribe to comments**:

Readers can subscribe to comments on a particular post by email or through their favorite RSS reader. If they have an IntenseDebate account, they also have the option to send a Twitter message or "Tweet" to alert their friends that they have commented on a particular post.

◆ **Reputation and voting**:

Another useful feature is the reputation system. Visitors can vote on comments, and comments that get a lot of negative votes will be hidden from view unless a user requests to see them. This is a handy form of "self moderation" for the community. The reputation system applies to only logged in users and gives each user an overall rating based on the quality of their comments on sites all over the Internet.

Activating IntenseDebate on your users' blogs

One important thing to remember is that even if you set IntenseDebate to automatically activate for your users, it won't do anything unless they set it up. Your users will still have the original WordPress MU comment system. They will be alerted to the fact that the plugin is not working for them by a message that will appear at the top of every page in their admin panel.

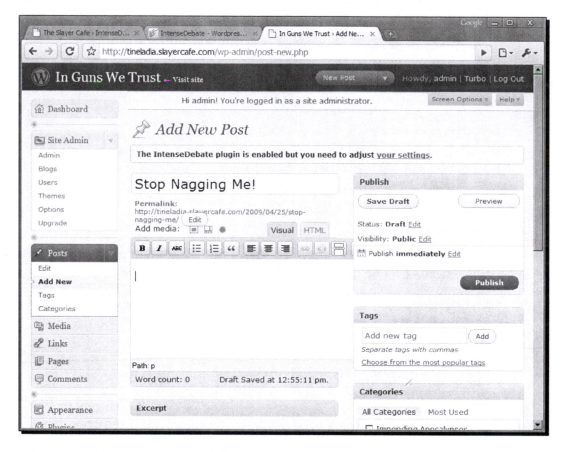

Have a go hero – tweaking IntenseDebate

IntenseDebate has so many features that there is not enough room to cover them all here.

Take a look at the Extras (`http://intensedebate.com/extras`) page for some widgets that you may want to add to your blog.

Also, check the **Settings** page for your blog in IntenseDebate. You can edit the moderation settings on that page. The default settings include a list of spam words that will cause comments to be flagged for moderation. Comments will also be flagged for moderation if they contain more than two URLs.

You can tweak the commenting system's settings to filter by IP address, email address, key words, and profanity. You can also alter how the comments are displayed, the text displayed when people report comments, the layout, and the location of the blog's RSS feed. You may want to change that to use the FeedBurner version of the RSS feed.

Community features—gravatars

Gravatars are **Globally Recognized Avatars**. They allow people to carry the same avatar from site to site without having to register at each site and take the time to upload an image.

Gravatars are supported by IntenseDebate by default. If a user has a gravatar and gives the email address that the gravatar is tied to when they make a comments, then the gravatar will be displayed beside that comment.

Since version 2.5, WordPress MU has had gravatar support built in. Let's add gravatars to our post pages.

Time for action – gravatars in WordPress MU

1. Open your theme's `index.php` file. In our case we are editing the Blue Zinfandel theme.

2. Find the section that begins with `<div class="contentdate">`.

3. Remove all markup up to the closing `</div>` tag and insert the following code:

```php
<?php

$email = $authordata->user_email;
$hash = md5($email);
$uri = 'http://www.gravatar.com/avatar/' . $hash . '?d=identicon&r
                                               =any&size=80';

$headers = wp_get_http_headers($uri);

if (!is_array($headers)) :
        echo "<h3>";
        echo the_time('M');
        echo "</h3><h4>";
        echo the_time('j');
        echo "</h4>";
```

```
elseif (isset($headers["content-disposition"]) ) :
        echo get_avatar( $authordata->user_email, $size = '50') ;
else :
        echo "<h3>";
        echo the_time('M');
        echo "</h3><h4>";
        echo the_time('j');
        echo "</h4>";
endif;

?>
```

4. Save and upload the file.

5. If you wish to use gravatars on user blogs, you will also need to edit the user's version of the theme file.

6. Now, if a post author has a gravatar, it will be displayed in the title section of their posts. If not, the default **Date of Post** box will appear instead.

What just happened?

We have used the built-in WordPress MU gravatars function to display a member's gravatar in the title section of any posts they make.

As the default **No Gravatar Set** image is rather boring, our code checks to see if the author in question has a gravatar. If the author does not, or if the Gravatars web site is not accessible for any reason, then we display the normal post date icon instead.

Gravatars provide a way for people to carry their identity from site to site. Showing a recognizable face for your site's authors builds recognition among readers and helps readers and blog authors to build a relationship with each other.

You might be wondering why the output in the previous code is broken into several `echo` statements. I have chosen that method purely because I find it more readable. You could save yourself some typing if you built an `echo` statement similar to this one:

```
echo "<h3>". the_time('M')."</h3>"
```

Have a go hero – gravatars and themes

The code used to edit the SlayerCafe blog theme was very simplistic. The theme you are using for your site may be structured differently.

In the theme for the SlayerCafe, the calendar icon that shows the date of the latest post is coded into the CSS file. The change I have made to the `index.php` file does not prevent the calendar icon from being loaded. The gravatar image simply loads over the top of it.

Try reworking the theme file to correct this. One way to do so would be to create a copy of the `contentdate` class in the `styles.css` file, which does not load the calendar image. Call the new class `contentgravatar` and then create different `<div>` tags to be displayed depending on whether you wish to show the calendar or the gravatar.

Encouraging sign-ups with downloads for members only

If you offer file downloads, restricting some of them to only members is a good way to encourage people to sign up. It is a good idea to offer some file downloads to visitors who are just passing through so that you can build up their trust, as some people are uncomfortable giving out their email address to an unknown web site. Also, some people do not want to take the time to register to download a file, especially if they don't know if it is going to be a worthwhile download.

A good compromise is to offer some files to everyone and other files for members only, or to offer some content on your blog and then a download in a more convenient form.

As an example, some of the Watchers on SlayerCafe could run tutorials about demon identification and slaying techniques. They may offer text and image versions as blog posts, with an MP3 version of the lesson that registered Slayers could download to listen to while they are on patrol. This is likely to have a high conversion rate in terms of registrations; the visiting Slayers will hopefully be impressed by the quality of the information in the tutorials and want to download the audio version.

One useful plugin that restricts downloads to registered users only is the User Only Downloads plugin available at `http://wpmudev.org/project/user-only-downloads`. This plugin is very easy to use. For some reason the author uploaded the plugin to WPMU Dev as a text file, so you will need to rename it to a `.php` file before you can use it. Just upload the renamed file to your `mu-plugins` folder and tell your users that they can restrict file downloads to members only by using the following tag in their posts:

```
[user_download URL]
```

Logged in users will see a download link, while everyone else will see a bold message telling them that they need to be logged in to download files.

Welcoming new visitors

Blog networks can be confusing when you first visit them. Why not ease the confusion a little by showing first-time visitors a special welcome message at the top of the page, which explains what the site is about and invites them to get involved in some way?

Time for action – creating a welcome message

1. Download the What Would Seth Godin Do plugin from `http://wordpress.org/extend/plugins/what-would-seth-godin-do/`.

2. Copy the `what_would_seth_godin_do.php` file to your `/wp-content/plugins` folder.

3. Activate the plugin in your admin panel.

4. Turn on auto-activation using Plugin Commander.

5. Go to **Settings | WWSGD** and add a welcome message for new members.

6. Leave the **Repetition** setting at the default (first 5 visits).

7. If you have something you would like to alert regular visitors of, you can use the **Message to Return Visitors** box.

8. I recommend testing the plugin with the **Location of Message** set to **Before Post**. If you don't like the location of the message, change the setting to use the template tag instead.

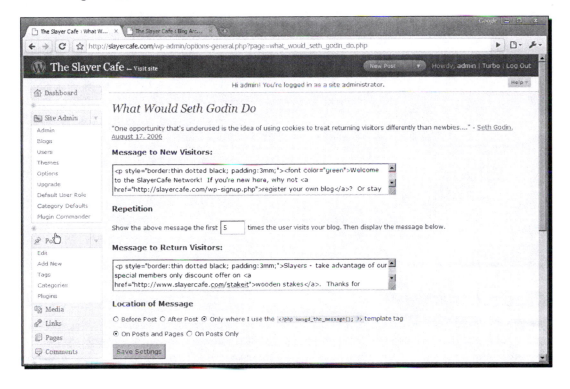

9. New visitors to your site should see a welcome message like this one:

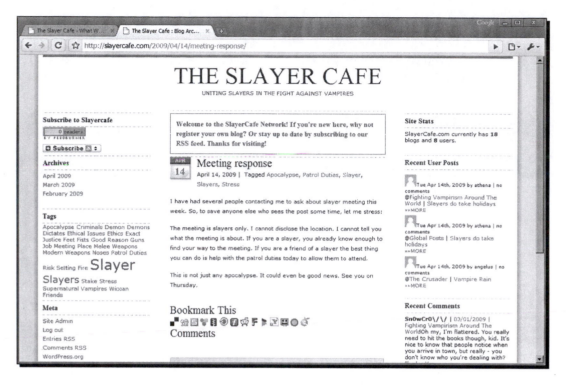

What just happened?

The What Would Seth Godin Do plugin uses cookies to distinguish between first-time visitors and regular visitors. You can use this knowledge to offer visitors a different experience depending on how many times they have visited the site.

If a visitor comes to your site via a link on someone else's blog, they may not realize that they are visiting a blog network and may not understand what the site is about. A simple message letting them know the subject of the site and inviting them to create their own blog or subscribe to the site's feed should help to point them in the right direction.

You may not want to show a message to returning visitors all the time, but if you have a promotion or special offer that you'd like to display prominently, then using the What Would Seth Godin Do plugin is a convenient way to do so.

The default **Before Post** setting did not work well for SlayerCafe, so I edited the `index.php` and `home.php` template files to get the welcome message to appear in the right place. For the theme I was using, the code `<?php wwsgd_the_message(); ?>` should be placed below the line that says `<div id="contentmiddle">`.

If you decide to use template tags to display the welcome message, don't forget to add the tags to all of the themes that you will be allowing your users to select.

Welcome message not showing up?

If you can't see the welcome message, you may need to clear your cookies, or at least delete the cookies for the blog network. Most browsers make it easy for you to find the cookies that belong to a particular site. For example, in Firefox just go to **Tools | Options**, click on the **Privacy** tab, and then click **Show Cookies.....** Use the search box to find the cookie you want to delete, select it, and click **Remove Cookie**.

See the following screenshots for a clearer idea of what you're looking for.

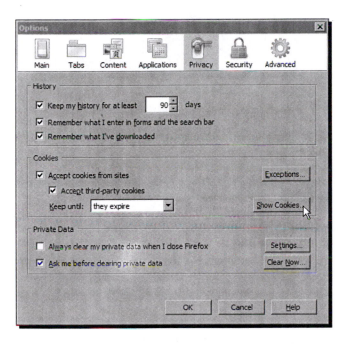

The Cookies screen allows you to see a list of all the cookies Firefox has stored, and you can find the cookies related to your site by using the search box.

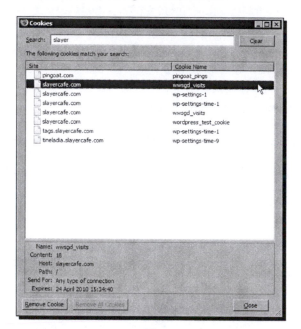

Related posts for visitors from search engines

If visitors arrive on your blog network via a search engine, it's likely that they are looking for some information about a specific topic.

Why not take advantage of that by showing search engine-referred visitors a list of posts related to the keywords they searched for?

One way to achieve this is to use the Search Engine Related Posts plugin available at `http://wordpress.org/extend/plugins/search-engine-related-posts/`. Just install the plugin as normal and then add the markup `<div style="display:none" id="search_content"></div>` to your theme files at the point where you want the list to appear. For most people, this would be after the post display section of their `index.php` file.

The plugin will check the referrer details of your visitors and only show a list of related posts to the people who have been referred by a search engine. This increases the chance of those visitors staying around to read more articles, finding what they need, and becoming a regular reader of your site.

Regular visitors are probably reading your blog to stay up to date with the latest news and don't need to see a list of links to older posts, as it is likely that they have already seen them.

Other ways to engage the community

The above are just a few ways you can engage your visitors. There are many others that you may want to look into. Here are a few for inspiration:

Polls

Allowing your members to create polls is a useful way to get feedback from your members and to add a little interactivity to the site. If your site's authors pick the right questions, the information gathered from the polls can be useful, too.

A good polls plugin is: `http://wpmudev.org/project/powpoll-for-wpmu-27`.

This is one of the easier plugins to get working with WordPress MU. Many of the standard WordPress poll plugins require several steps to activate them on each member's blog, but PoWPoll can be set to automatically activate on new blogs.

The plugin supports voting restrictions, such as one vote per IP address, and restricts vote casting to logged-in visitors.

Sitewide searching

Making it easy for your visitors to find the content they are looking for is an important part of making a sticky site. With a niche blogging network, it is likely that someone who is interested in the posts of one member will also be interested in the posts of others. They may want to search for posts on a specific topic contained anywhere within the network.

There are a number of ways you could implement a sitewide search feature. There are some plugins, such as One Search (`http://jason.ungos.com/projects/one-search-wpmu-plugin/`), that tie in to WordPress MU to allow sitewide searching, or you could use Google's Site Search.

One Search requires that the user who is accessing the WordPress MU database has the rights to create VIEWS. At the time of writing, the code available on the plugin author's web site will also need to be tweaked to work with WordPress MU versions 2.7.1 and above.

It is possible to integrate Google Custom Search Engine so that the results page fits with your template. You can learn more at `http://www.google.com/coop/cse/`.

Pop quiz – doing the thing

1. What do people mean by "sticky"?
   a) A web site that is difficult to navigate, so it takes you ages to find things you need.
   b) A web site that engages readers, making them want to return.
   c) A web site that takes a long time to download, so it makes the browser "stick".

2. What are gravatars?
   a) Graphical Avatars.
   b) Graphic, Realistic Avatars.
   C) Globally Recognized Avatars.

Answers: (1) b, (2) c.

Summary

This chapter covered ways to make your site sticky so that when you attract new visitors, they stay around and become part of the community.

We learned about using contact forms to make it easy for our visitors to contact us, and adding a more personal feel to blog posts through the use of gravatars. We also learned about comments and how to make the discussion that takes place in the comments sections of our blogs easier to follow through rating, threaded discussions, and subscription options.

We discussed the value of related posts links to help our visitors find posts that may interest them, and we talked about using polls and searches to draw users in to the site encouraging them to explore everything the site has to offer and making them feel like a part of the community.

We also discussed some other ways to improve the experience for both new and regular visitors, including displaying different messages to new visitors to help them "find their feet" on the site.

So far, we've looked at ways to encourage readers to engage with the authors who own blogs on our site. This is a good way to build regular readers. Many people enjoy joining in with discussions on the Internet, but do not want to run their own blog—perhaps because they don't have the time to commit to writing on a regular basis. Such people may still want to discuss issues relating to our site's niche in more depth, however, and so our next chapter will look at adding forums to our network. That way, bigger discussions can take place in one central location instead of being spread out across various blog comment sections.

Adding Forums with bbPress

So far, we have given our visitors the chance to share their thoughts in the form of comments on other people's blogs and through the creation of their own blogs, but sometimes blogging is not the best way to carry out a conversation. Perhaps the visitor in question doesn't want to commit to running a blog in the long term, or perhaps they want a more in-depth conversation rather than a quick back-and-forth in the comments section of a blog post. That's where forums come in.

In this chapter we will:

- ◆ Set up the bbPress forum script
- ◆ Learn how to integrate the bbPress script with WordPress MU
- ◆ Learn how to change the style of the forums
- ◆ Learn how to moderate the forums
- ◆ Take a look at some of the interesting plugins available for bbPress

So let's get on with it...

Installing bbPress

To install bbPress, you will need some information about your WordPress MU setup. It's a good idea to have your wpmu-config.php file opened and be logged in to your WordPress MU admin panel, so you can find all the information you need quickly and easily.

There are a lot of forum scripts that can be made to work with WordPress MU through the use of some creative coding, including the ever popular phpBB. However, for the purposes of this book we will use bbPress, as it is designed for use with WordPress and WordPress MU, and it offers easy cookie and theme integration, as well as the ability to share account information between the two scripts. bbPress is used to power WordPress.org's own support forums, as well as the forums for several other large communities including Automattic and Technorati. This means when your community grows, you can be confident that bbPress will be able to keep up! Also, bbPress has a lot of out of the box nice features, including spam protection and support for gravatars.

Time for action – installing bbPress

1. Download bbPress from `http://bbpress.org/`.

2. Extract the archive and upload the contents to the location you want bbPress to be installed to. I chose `/bbpress` in the root folder of the web site, but you can choose a different location if you wish.

3. Using your web browser, go to the address where you have uploaded bbPress. You should see a screen like this:

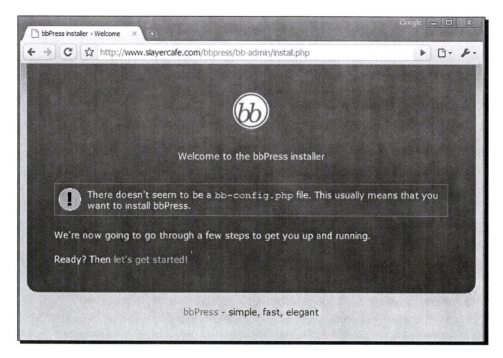

4. Click **let's get started!**

5. On the next screen, enter the name of your WordPress MU database, along with the username and password you use to connect to it. You can find the database connection details in the `wpmu-config.php` file.

6. Most people won't need to change anything in the advanced settings section. However, if your database is not on the same server as the rest of your web site, you can enter the database server's address by clicking **Show Advanced Settings** and replacing **localhost** with the correct address.

7. On the next screen you will need to enter the secret keys and salts that WordPress MU is using—you can find them in the `wp-config.php` file. You should also tick **Add user database integration settings**. Leave the user database table prefix unchanged, unless you know you changed the table that WordPress MU installed to. Finally, you will be asked to nominate an admin user, or keymaster.

8. You have now finished the setup process. Your forum should look something like this:

Unable to create bb-config.php?

If you get an error message saying that the setup script was unable to create the `bb-config.php` file, just change the file permissions for the `bbpress` folder to 777, using either the `chmod` command or your FTP client. If you need to do this, be sure to set the permissions back to 755 once the setup process is complete.

What just happened?

We have installed bbPress and set up the user databases so that users need only one set of login details for both the forum and the blog. This works because bbPress has access to the WordPress MU database. At this moment in time, our users will need to log in twice—once for the forum and once for the blog. But they will need to remember only one set of login details.

Fortunately, this can be corrected by sharing some cookie information. We will do this next.

Running bbPress from other folders/subdomains

It is possible to configure bbPress to run from any folder you wish. If you do this, remember that you will need to change any path references seen later in this chapter to reflect the location you installed bbPress to. You can also make bbPress run from a subdomain; we will look at this later in the chapter.

One login for both the forum and the blog

If you log in to bbPress using your keymaster user, you should see a list of currently registered users on the dashboard. This list will include all currently registered WordPress MU users.

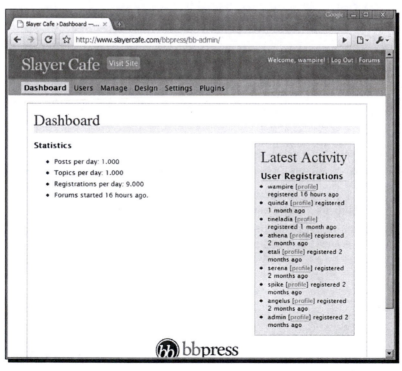

You may have noticed that the bbPress admin page somewhat resembles the admin page of WordPress MU. You should find most of the bbPress admin functions to be fairly intuitive.

While existing blog users will be copied over to bbPress without requiring any admin intervention, the same cannot be said for the reverse. If a user registers on the forums, they are given an entry in the WordPress MU user list, but the new user has no roles assigned to them. A similar situation arises with new blog users—they can create a blog, but they are unable to use the forums. This can cause problems and confusion for your users. Let's start by ensuring that our users only have to enter their login details once, to get logged in to the entire site.

Time for action – user DB integration with WordPress MU

1. Download and install the following WordPress plugins—the bbPress Integration plugin (available at `http://wordpress.org/extend/plugins/bbpress-integration/`) and WPMU Enable bbPress Capabilities (available at `http://bbpress.org/plugins/topic/wpmu-enable-bbpress-capabilities/`).

2. Log in to the bbPress admin panel and go to **Settings | WordPress Integration**.

3. Open your `wp-config.php` file and paste the following lines of code into it, replacing the domain name with your own:

   ```
   define('COOKIE_DOMAIN', '.slayercafe.com');
   define('COOKIEPATH', '/');
   ```

4. Go to **Settings | WordPress Integration** in the bbPress admin panel and scroll down to the bottom of the page. Look for the `$bb->authcookie` entry. Remove the `wordpress_` prefix from the value and add the following code to your `wp-config` file, inserting the cookie value in the relevant place:

   ```
   define('COOKIEHASH', 'cookie value_goes_here' );
   ```

5. Try logging in to the main blog and then navigating to the forums. If you find that you are not automatically logged in to bbPress, continue to the next step.

6. Back up your `wp-config.php` file.

7. Delete all the key and hash values from `wp-config.php`. Then, log in to your admin panel; you should see a yellow warning box at the screen with some new keys in it. Copy these, and paste them back into your `wp-config.php` file.

8. Back up `bb-config.php`.

9. Open `bb-config.php` and paste the values in there as well. However, prefix each name with BB, as shown next:

```
define( 'BB_NONCE_KEY', 'Bx(wloghv1HNDT$^67&mQd4G' );
define( 'BB_AUTH_KEY', 'qHf&FTERgcOIyKb44Ar0dk@E' );
define( 'BB_AUTH_SALT', '5)7DnTI@ilIGq4Dh$OQ4Cg%I' );
define( 'BB_LOGGED_IN_KEY', '9sFsCZ4D3o)Lucbtj8IOS0wl' );
define( 'BB_LOGGED_IN_SALT', 'M7Mn#^4jdkLj7@K!e@8vRuS6' );
define( 'BB_SECURE_AUTH_KEY', 'J)KvT$4Zn%(hx1#55uusPfC1' );
define( 'BB_SECURE_AUTH_SALT', 'zix@wNP8m$LChB&29Ica^FEH' );
```

10. Now, logging in to the forums should also log you in to the blog, and vice versa.

Keep your keys secret!

The key values used in this book are not the same as the values that are in use on the SlayerCafe site. They are older values, left in just to give you an idea of what the keys are supposed to look like. It is best to keep your keys and salts secret. If you need to make a support request on the WordPress MU or bbPress forums, change your key to say "nonce-key-value-in-here" or something similar.

What just happened?

We have set up bbPress so that it uses the same cookie information as WordPress. A cookie is a text file that web sites use to track your browsing activity. Cookies are also one of the ways for the web sites to identify you. Many web sites store a portion of your login details in a cookie so that they know who you are when you return to the site.

WordPress encrypts the details in cookies for security reasons. We gave bbPress the information it needs to know to be able to understand the cookie and create cookies that WordPress can also understand.

Handling new users

Now, let's handle the issue of new user registrations, to make sure that when a user registers, they get access to both the forum and the blog network.

Time for action – blog and forum registrations

1. Check the default user role that you assign to new users. If you are using the Default User Role or Role Manager plugins, this may be different from the standard Administrator/editor roles.

2. Log in to the bbPress admin panel and go to **Settings | WordPress Integration**.

3. Use the User Role Map settings to assign WordPress MU user roles to new users who register on the forums. A standard new user would be a member. If you want to offer elevated privileges to moderators or revoke blogging rights for blocked users, you can set different rights for such users.

4. Now, try registering through the blogs and through the forums. Make sure that each account has access to everything it needs on the blog network.

What just happened?

We have made our final tweak to make sure that from a user's perspective, registration and login is seamless. Now, users will be able to sign up from either part of the site and have the login details work across the whole site. Of course, if a user joins on the forums, they will not automatically be assigned a blog, but they will be able to set one up later if desired.

Seamless theme integration

Unless you are creating a web site about a new product or subject—for example, an unreleased computer game or a relatively unknown actor—the chances are that there are already dozens, if not hundreds of the sites competing for your visitors.

One way to set your site apart from all the others is to have a professional appearance. Anyone can install a couple of scripts and stick a free theme on each one. It's easy to tell if that's all the webmaster has done because the site looks like a frankensite—an ugly monster of a site made from several different scripts that don't always fit well together.

If you spend some time making your site blend together, your visitors will see that you have taken your site seriously. Your site will stand out from the ones that have just been thrown together and will inspire confidence in your visitors.

Fortunately, it is possible to share theme information between WordPress MU and bbPress, so you can blend your forum and your blog network together without needing to create a new design from scratch.

Time for action – styling your forum

1. Open `bb-config.php` and add the following line (replacing PATHTOYOUR with the relative path to your blog):

```
require_once('/PATHTOYOUR/wp-blog-header.php');
```

2. Navigate to the folder for the theme you are using on the forum (the default is Kakumei, which is in `/bb-templates/kakumei`) and open the `header.php` file. Replace the contents with `<?php get_header(); ?>`.

3. After the `<?php get_header(); ?>`, insert the following line of code:

```
<link rel="stylesheet" href="<?php bb_stylesheet_uri(); ?>"
type="text/css" />.
```

4. You can do the same with the footer, replacing it with `<?php get_footer(); ?>` if you wish.

5. Open the `style.css` file for the bbPress theme you are using. Search for the following line in the header: class.

```
background: url('images/page_header_bblogo.png') no-repeat
```

Remove that line and save the file.

6. View the forum. It should now be very similar in look and feel to the rest of the blog network.

What just happened?

bbPress uses its own theme system. Some WordPress themes have bbPress counterparts, but not all of them. We have managed to make our bbPress site look like it is using the same theme as the rest of the site by replacing the contents of the bbPress header file with a call to the WordPress MU `get_header` function. This loads the header of our active WordPress MU theme.

We have added a link to the bbPress stylesheet so that the rest of the page is styled correctly—for example, the correct fonts and background colors are applied to the listings of threads and posts.

This works well for the Blue Zinfandel theme. However, with some other themes you may find that the WordPress CSS file and the bbPress CSS file conflict with each other. In this case, you can fix the problem by creating a custom CSS file for bbPress and telling bbPress to load that instead of the WordPress MU stylesheet.

If you would like to learn more about CSS, the following resources are a good starting point:

+ `http://www.w3schools.com/`
+ `http://www.w3.org/Style/CSS/learning`
+ `http://www.html.net/tutorials/CSS/introduction.asp`

Have a go hero – more advanced styling and integration

At this moment, our visitors are presented with a login message at the top of the forum, but this message takes them to the WordPress MU login screen. When they enter their details, they will be taken to the WordPress MU dashboard instead of to the forum.

This is rather confusing, and it would be much better if the login link in the header was different depending on where you were on the site such that the main site's login link would take you to the WordPress MU login page, and the forum's link would take you to the bbPress login page.

The address for the bbPress login page is `http://www.slayercafe.com/bbpress/bb-login.php`.

You can change what is displayed in the header by setting a flag inside the bbPress header file before you call the WordPress `get_header()` function. You can also rely on the `$bb` global variable that is used by bbPress. However, I suggest making your own flag, just in case bbPress ever changes its variable names.

Put some code like this at the start of the `header.php` file of bbPress:

```
<?php global $onforum;
$onforum = TRUE; ?>
```

Then in the WordPress MU's `header.php` file, you can use some `if` statements to display different content depending on where the page is being loaded from. You could use this to change the title tags and display different links in the header.

Managing your forum

Now that the forum is nicely tied in with the rest of the site, let's populate it with a few sections and assign moderator jobs to some of our trusted staff.

Time for action – managing your forum

1. To create new forum sections, go to **Manage | Forums** in the bbPress admin panel.

2. Creating new forum sections is simply a case of entering a section name, and, optionally a description:

3. A forum section with no parent assigned is a top-level forum. If you assign a parent, then the section will be listed as a subforum of the parent.

4. If you tick **Forum is Category**, then the forum will serve as a parent but won't be able to accept any posts itself:

5. If you want to change a forum you have created, just click **Edit** next to that forum on the **Manage** page. If you want to reorder the forums, just click the **Edit Forum Order** button, drag the forum you want to move, and then click **Save Forum Order**. Note that only the forum you have selected will be moved. So, if you want to move any related child sections, you will need to do those separately.

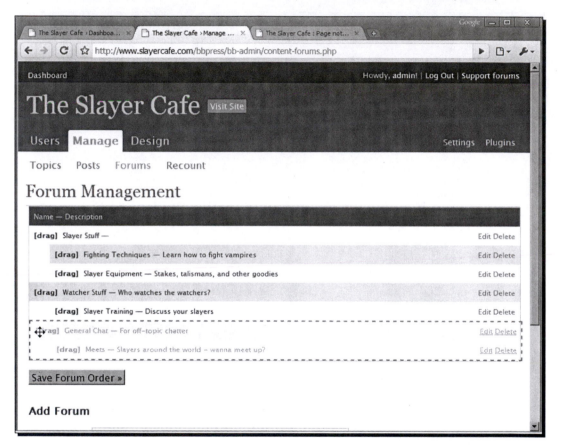

What just happened?

We have set up several different forums so that our site's users can easily find the kinds of posts they are looking for. Slayers can talk to other Slayers in the Slayer Stuff forums, with special sections for fighting techniques and for sourcing equipment. Watchers have their own dedicated area where they can discuss more academic matters without Slayers confusing things with their youthful enthusiasm.

For now, we have made only a handful of forums. As the site grows, we can add more. It is a good idea to choose just a couple of forum headings when you create your site. If you have a huge list of topics but only a post or two under each one, then your site looks empty, which does not inspire people to join. Remember that you can always expand your forums if you find that there is a need to do so.

With SlayerCafe, we found that it did not take long for the Wiccan members to request their own private forum. When the site's forums were first created, the Wiccans and the Slayers both used the Slayer Stuff section. During the early days of the site, there were just a couple of Wiccans, so this was not an issue for the Slayers. When the site became popular with Slayers outside the United Kingdom, the number of Wiccans increased dramatically and this caused tension between the Slayers and the Wiccans. The Slayers wanted places to discuss secret issues, and the Wiccans wanted somewhere to discuss spells without the Slayers questioning the safety of their magic every few posts. Adding an extra section was an easy task to do and made both groups very happy, thereby earning free positive publicity in the process!

Managing your users

Now that we have someplace for our users to post, we need to make sure that the posts that our users make are on topic and of a good quality. We need to keep our community free of spam, illegal content, and possibly **flame bait** (posts made with the intent of angering members—for example, someone registering on SlayerCafe and saying that Vampires are actually good guys and Slayers are murderers).

One person can't moderate a forum 24/7, so we need to have a team of moderators. Moderating a forum requires different skills to managing a blog network, and you may not trust your moderators with access to some of the commands found in the backend of WordPress MU. The good news is that you don't have to. You can set permissions for bbPress separately, giving your moderator team access to only the features that they need.

Time for action – setting user permissions

1. Log in to the bbPress admin panel, and go to **Users**.

2. The admin account is listed under **Key Master**, whereas other accounts are in the **Member** section.

3. Click **Edit** next to the member that you would like to promote or demote.

User List by Role

1 – 3 of 3 shown below

Key Master

ID	Username	Display name	Email	Registered Since	Actions
1	admin	admin	etali@myth-games.com	2009-05-09 13:51:40	Edit

Member

ID	Username	Display name	Email	Registered Since	Actions
2	tineladia	tineladia	comps@myth-games.com	2009-05-09 19:33:42	Edit
3	wampy	wampy	admin@myth-games.com	2009-05-09 20:19:07	Edit

4. On the next screen, you can change the user's permissions. I plan to promote Tineladia to the administrator position and make Wampy a moderator. You can have more than one user in each role if you wish:

5. Below the **User Type** dropdown is an option to allow users to ignore the 30 second post throttling limit. I have ticked this for the users that I am promoting.

6. Now your promoted users should be able to edit and delete posts, and should have limited access to the admin panel.

Password strength—missing jQuery?

To show a password strength indicator on the edit profile page, you will need to use the JavaScript library, jQuery. This comes with bbPress and can be found in the `bb-includes/js/jquery` folder. I have chosen not to use this as it can cause performance problems in older browsers, but adding a reference to the location of the script in the header file of your theme will enable it if you do want to use it.

What just happened?

We have promoted a few of our users so that they can edit and delete posts and access some more features in the admin panel. Our promoted users will be able to watch over the blog while we aren't online and hopefully keep it free of spammers, trolls (of both the Internet and mythical variety), and other undesirables.

You may have noticed some other user roles such as **Inactive** and **Blocked**. These may be suitable for users that you would like to ban temporarily. Users with those roles are not able to interact with other members of the site, but their account is still in the database. So, if you ever want to restore their rights, you can. This could be useful if a Slayer temporarily turns evil—her Watcher could lock her out of the site by putting her in one of the limited user groups until they find a way to convert her back to the side of good.

Useful plugins for bbPress

The basic bbPress setup is functional, but it lacks a number of basic features users may be accustomed to from having used other forums. Fortunately, these can be added using plugins.

Time for action – installing plugins

The bbPress plugin system is very similar to the WordPress MU plugin system, so you should find it pretty intuitive to use.

1. Download the plugin from `bbpress.org`. Let's start with a humanizer plugin to prevent spam registrations. The plugin can be obtained from `http://bbpress.org/plugins/topic/human-test/`.

2. Extract the plugin and upload the files to the `/bb-plugins` folder.

3. Go to **Manage | Plugins** in your bbPress admin panel and activate your new plugin. While you're there, you may want to activate the **Akismet** anti-spam plugin and the **Bozo Users** plugin.

4. Don't forget to add your API key under the **Akismet Configuration** tab to take advantage of the Akismet spam-blocking features.

5. The Human Test for bbPress plugin adds a simple question to the registration page, which should prevent bots from being able to sign up.

What just happened?

We have just installed our first bbPress plugin. There are several plugins available for bbPress. You can find a list of those at `http://bbpress.org/plugins/`.

Most forum users will want, at the very least, private messaging, signatures, and the ability to use BBCode to make their posts more attractive. It is not safe from an administrator's perspective to allow users to add HTML to their posts. Therefore, BBCode was created to allow forum users to customize their posts in a more secure way—for example, by making text bold or italic, or by adding links and images. You can read more about BBCode at `http://en.wikipedia.org/wiki/BBCode`.

Depending on the kind of community you wish to run, you may want to add a few of the plugins listed on the bbPress plugins page. Some of the best ones include:

- **bbRatings**: Allows users to give star ratings to topics.
- **Allow Images**: Allows users to post images.
- **BBCode Lite**: Allows the use of BBCode in posts. This plugin offers better performance than most other BBCode plugins.
- **Simple OnlineList**: Allows you to add a list of recently active users to the bottom of your forum.
- **bbPress Signatures**: Allows users to set a signature, which will display at the end of their posts.
- **Private Messaging**: Adds private messaging functionality to the forum.
- **Hidden Forums**: Allows you to create forums that can only be seen by certain types of people—for example, registered users, moderators, or administrators.
- **Post Count Plus**: A plugin to display a user's post count next to their posts.
- **bbTrack**: Tracks users and bots as they navigate around the site.
- **bbPolls**: Allows users to attach polls to their posts.
- **Moderation Suite**: Adds tools for users to report posts and to help moderators perform their duties.

There are many other useful plugins, but the above are some of the most flexible and most popular. I'd recommend at least the use of the Bozo's plugin as a way to punish abusive users. This plugin can be used to send people to Coventry—they can make posts, but nobody else can see them, so they'll feel like everyone is ignoring them. On SlayerCafe, suspected trolls (for example, Vampires who register to try to stir up trouble among the Slayers) will be moderated using the Bozo feature. Watchers will check on Bozo posts from time to time, ban those who are repeat offenders, and promote those who clean up their act.

If you add the plugins that you feel you need, you should find that the forum starts to look a little more fully featured.

However, you may find that you need to tweak the theme files to get everything to appear in the right place, especially if you are using your WordPress MU theme's header and footer. Fortunately, in most cases the edits are fairly simple.

Have a go hero – sharing information between forum and blog

Why not set up bbSync so that posts made to the announcement category of the main blog will be published to the forum? The Watchers on SlayerCafe will be using that feature to ensure that the maximum number of users see important announcements about meetings, vampire attacks, and interesting discoveries.

In my experience, once you set up the forum, you may find that most people spend their time there, and perhaps on the blogs of their friends. They will expect people to tell them about important announcements that come from the site owners and will forget to check the owner's blogs themselves. The more ways you offer for your users to stay up to date with important information, the better!

Displaying recent posts in your blog

To encourage users to visit your forum, why not promote the most recent posts in your sidebar? This is made easy to do thanks to a WordPress plugin called Latest-bb-Posts in WordPress, which can be downloaded from `http://wordpress.org/extend/plugins/bbpress-latest-discussion/`.

If you want to exclude forums from the list for any reason, you can do this by editing the SQL statement in the plugin file—just add the clause AND NOT IN, along with the forum number you want to exclude.

Creating forum topics using blog posts

Another useful feature is to automatically have forum topics created from blog posts. If you decide to use a plugin that offers this, you should set it up only on the main blog. At the time of writing, this could be accomplished using the bbSync plugin, which can be downloaded from the `bbpress.org` web site; however, there are plans to have this feature implemented in bbPress itself in a future version.

Pop quiz – doing the thing

1. bbPress is:
    a) A "lite" version of WordPress.
    b) A forum script designed to run in text-only mode, like the old Bulletin Board services.
    c) A forum script created by the WordPress developers for users with WordPress and WordPress MU.

2. bbPress plugins go:
    a) In `/wp-content/plugins`
    b) In `/wp-content/mu-plugins`
    c) In `/bbpress`
    d) In `/bbpress/bb-plugins`
    e) There are no plugins for bbPress

3. Your secret keys and salts:
    a) Are the same as the keys and salts everyone else has.
    b) Are randomly generated and not really that important—it's fine to run WordPress MU without having any set up.
    c) Are randomly generated and are used as an extra layer of security. It's a good idea to set them, and you should keep them secret.

    Answers: (1) c, (2) d, (3) c

We have touched on some of the most interesting and useful features of bbPress and how it can be made to tie in to WordPress MU, but there are many more features you could explore. It is well worth exploring `bbPress.org` to see what others have done with their sites; hopefully, you will find some inspiration that will help in the development of your community!

Summary

This chapter covered a few of the things that you can do with bbPress. We will revisit bbPress in later chapters as we continue to add even more features to the blog network. For now, you should have a working forum that relies on your WordPress MU user information, and the forum and the blog network should blend seamlessly with each other.

This chapter barely scratched the surface of what BuddyPress can do. We learned how to install the software and how to share cookies with WordPress MU so that our users need to log in only once to access the whole site. We also learned how to style BuddyPress so that it matches the rest of the blog and how to manage registrations so that spam bots cannot register on the site.

We learned about moderation and setting user roles so that we can assign moderators to various parts of the forum.

We also discussed some useful plugins that extend the capabilities of bbPress to allow for polls, user-rating of posts, and improved moderation features. We also looked at some more advanced integration features such as altering the header display so that it displays different links depending on where the user is visiting from and displaying recent forum posts in the WordPress MU sidebar.

There are lots of other things that you can do with bbPress. We will look at some of those things in the next few chapters, as we expand our blog network to be even more social with the help of BuddyPress.

If you're not familiar with BuddyPress, it is a social networking script that ties in to WordPress MU and bbPress, allowing you to create a fully featured social networking site. With BuddyPress, our Slayers can maintain friend lists, photo galleries, and status feeds, and they can create groups where to keep track of each other's activities. The next chapter will give you an overview of what BuddyPress is and how to set it up.

9
Social Networking with BuddyPress

So far, we have set up a blog network and have given our users the chance to communicate with each other through blogs and forums. In this chapter, we will add some more social features in the form of the BuddyPress plugins.

In this chapter we will:

- ◆ Set up BuddyPress
- ◆ Change the BuddyPress themes
- ◆ Allow users to log in with Facebook Connect
- ◆ Add some Twitter features to our BuddyPress site
- ◆ Learn how to improve the performance of BuddyPress on our server

So let's get on with it...

BuddyPress

BuddyPress is a collection of WordPress MU plugins designed for social networking. Unlike the majority of the plugins we have used so far throughout this book, BuddyPress only works with WordPress MU, and not with the single-user version of WordPress—after all, a social networking site with only one blog to be used by all the members would not be very useful!

BuddyPress is actually a collection of plugins and it allows you to add a lot of features to your site, including extended profiles, private messaging, friends lists, groups, a messaging system called "The Wire" (which works in a similar fashion to "walls" on popular social networking sites), and an activity stream similar to the status update facilities on sites such as Twitter and Facebook.

Setting up BuddyPress

BuddyPress works just like a normal WordPress MU plugin, so the setup process should be familiar to you. You can download BuddyPress from `http://buddypress.org/download/`. The ZIP file contains the full suite of BuddyPress plugins and, once you've installed the suite, you can pick and choose the plugins that you want to use.

Time for action – installing the BuddyPress suite

1. Upload the contents of the BuddyPress archive to `/wp-content/plugins/`.

2. Move the `/wp-content/plugins/buddypress/bp-themes/` folder up to `/wp-content/bp-themes`.

3. Enable the BuddyPress plugin in your WordPress MU **Site Admin** panel.

4. Now go to the BuddyPress section of the admin panel—it should be listed on the left-hand side of the navigation bar.

5. You should be able to leave most of the defaults on the **BuddyPress Settings** page unchanged, although you may want to alter the default gravatar and change the **Base profile group name** to something meaningful.

6. The **Component Setup** page allows you to turn on and off individual BuddyPress components. We want to use them all on SlayerCafe, so we won't make any changes on this screen.

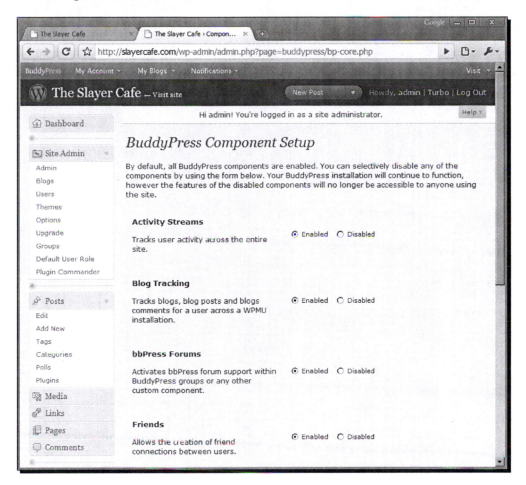

7. We now need to set up the forum membership. On the **Forums Setup** page, enter the URL you used for your bbPress forums. For most people, this will be `http://SITEADDRESS.COM/bbpress`.

8. Enter the username and password of the keyholder account.

9. Scroll down and tick **Turn on caching of requests to reduce latency and load**.

10. Now, your BuddyPress install should be ready to go. At the top of your browser window, you should see a new BuddyPress Admin Bar. Go to **My Account | Profile | My Profile**. You should see a page like this one:

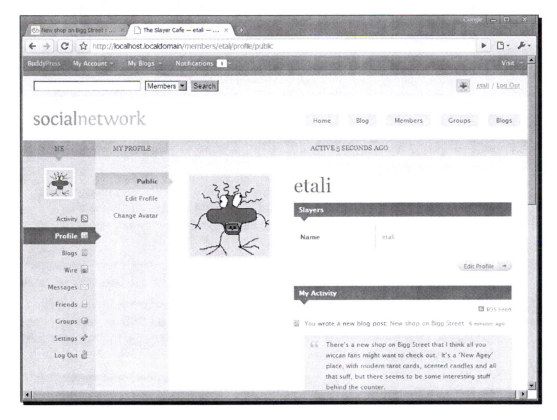

What just happened?

BuddyPress is a suite of WordPress MU plugins. We have just set up the basics, which will allow our registered and logged in users to feel more engaged with the site and with each other. As we work through this chapter, we will look at ways to improve the existing BuddyPress features and to better integrate BuddyPress with the rest of our site.

BuddyPress plugins explained

There are nine plugins in the base BuddyPress suite. Each one can be used to add a social feature to your site. The plugins are:

- **Extended Profiles**: This allows you to create extra profile fields, which can be filled in by the members.

- **Private Messaging**: This allows members to contact each other directly. There are private messaging plugins for WordPress and also for BuddyPress (which we will learn more about later). Rather than confusing your users with multiple places to send/receive PMs, I recommend testing each plugin and using the one that you feel best suits your site.

- **Friends**: This allows members to maintain friend lists, as they would on sites such as Facebook or MySpace.

- **Groups**: This allows members to create groups where they can post images, links, and blog posts. For example, Wicca practitioners could create a group to share spells, and Slayers from Los Angeles could have a group where they would share tips and news.

- **The Wire**: This plugin works like walls on other social networking sites. You can add a wire to a page or component, and users will be able to post messages to that page.

- **Activity Streams**: This plugin tracks member activity across the site. A member's activity stream will show new posts they have made, changes to their profile, and changes to their friends list. Members will also be able to keep up to date with their friends' activities via their stream.

- **Blog Tracking**: This feature aggregates all of the blogs, blog posts, and comments created by a specific member, making it easier for people to keep up with the blogging activities of their friends.

- **Forums**: This component allows groups to create and manage their own forums, using the existing bbPress plugin.

Future releases of BuddyPress are expected to have status updates—similar to Twitter updates and Facebook status feeds and photo albums.

Working with Extended Profiles

The default profile settings just ask for the name of the user. The chances are most members of your community would want to know more than that about their fellow users. Most SlayerCafe members, for example, would like to know if they're talking to a fellow Slayer, a Watcher, or some other demon-killing specialist. They'd also like to know if the people posting about vampire attacks live nearby, so they know if they can help in the fight.

The Extended Profiles feature allows you to set up custom profile fields designed for that purpose. There are some predefined fields for popular options such as "Country", and creating your own field is just a matter of choosing a name for the field, adding a description, and setting the type of the field. If you're using a drop-down box or a checkbox, you'll need to set the options that will appear in the list.

Private Messaging

The Private Messaging feature allows users to send private messages to each other. This feature is easy to use. Normal users have access to an **Inbox**, where they can read messages they have received. There is also a **Sent Messages** page where they can look through old messages they have sent and a **Compose** page where they can create messages to send to members.

Administrators have an extra option on the compose page and an extra page in their **My Messages** section. The extra option is a checkbox that says **This is a notice to all users**. Administrators can send sitewide messages and also review old messages they have sent in the **Notices** section.

Users will receive an email when someone sends them a private message. If they do not want to receive emails about new messages, they can turn off the notification option on the **Settings** page.

Friends list

The friends list feature enables members of your site to connect to each other. Users can add new friends by either searching for them on the **Friends** page or by clicking the **Add Friend** button on the profile page of their prospective friend. When they do this, the other user will receive a friend request and can either accept it or ignore it.

In the current version of BuddyPress, friends lists can be browsed by other members, and there are no privacy options to restrict this or the browsing of profiles.

Groups

Groups work just like the group features on Facebook and LinkedIn. Groups can have their own Wire attached to them for streams of general comments.

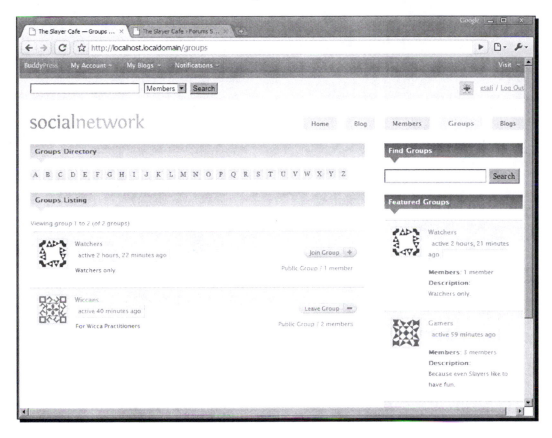

Groups can also have their own forums, which can be posted to via the bbPress part of the site or via the group's page. This allows for both general alerts and more in-depth threaded discussions. Group members can see a list of others who are also members of the group, making it easier for people with similar interests to connect.

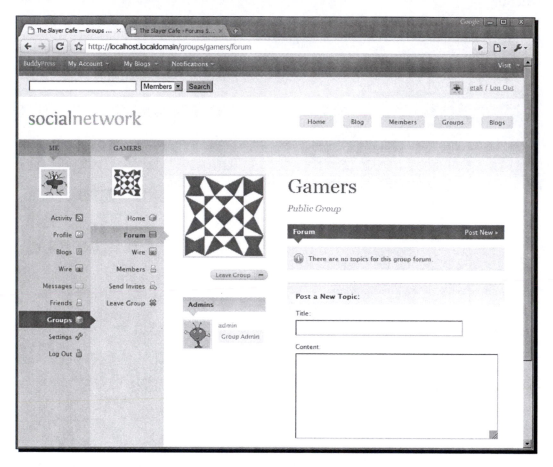

The Wire

The Wire works in the same way **walls and message boards** do on other social networking sites. Users can either write messages on their own Wires or they can leave messages on another user's Wire if they are friends with that user.

Users will be notified by email when a member posts on their Wire. If they do not want to receive notifications about this, they can turn off the notification option on the **Settings** page.

Wires don't have to be attached to users. When you (or a user) create a group, you can add a Wire to that too. Wires can be attached to almost any BuddyPress component, offering something similar to a guestbook or comments page functionality.

Activity streams

The activity stream contains updates of a user's activity around your site. Users can also view a stream that contains a list of their friend's activity. The activity stream can be posted to by any BuddyPress component so that blog posts, friend requests, wire posts, and other activities can be recorded there. Third-party components are also able to write to the activity stream if they wish.

Blog tracking

The blog tracking feature makes it a lot easier for your users to keep up to date with the blogging activities of people on their friends list. As WordPress MU allows multiple users per blog and multiple blogs per user, fans of a particular member may find it hard to keep up with their activities. For example; a younger, more "in touch" Watcher may make some very interesting posts on his own blog and also on the Watcher's dedicated blog, but would a young Slayer really want to have to search through all the stuffy and boring posts on the Watchers' blog to find the gems posted by this one particular user?

The Blog Tracking page aggregates all the posts that a user has made into one page and all the comments that the user has made into another page. There's even an RSS feed option so that users can subscribe to blog posts made by that particular member.

Forums

In Chapter 8, we set up bbPress so that it integrated seamlessly with WordPress MU. BuddyPress also ties in with WordPress MU. Groups created by users with sufficient privileges will automatically have their own forums created, and users can post to the bbPress forums either via the bbPress interface or via BuddyPress.

Forum integration not working?

If you can't get the bbPress integration to work with BuddyPress, double-check that your forums are set up correctly. You will find the instructions for this in Chapter 8. Also, check that you entered the forum path correctly and that the user you gave in the BuddyPress forum setup page has sufficient privileges.

Themes for your BuddyPress network

Just like WordPress MU, BuddyPress has a large number of themes available for it, and the number of themes you can choose from is growing rapidly. The BuddyPress developers have made it very easy for people to make new themes, and they have even provided a skeleton theme for would-be theme makers to work with.

You can download some new themes from the following sites:

- `http://www.buddydress.com/`
- `http://www.freebpthemes.com/`
- `http://wpmu.org/buddypress-themes-and-plugins/`

Time for action – installing new themes

Installing new themes is a fairly simple process:

1. Download your chosen theme. For SlayerCafe, we are using the facebuddy theme.

2. Extract the ZIP file and upload it to the `/wp-content/bp-themes` folder.

3. Enable the theme in the BuddyPress settings section of your WordPress MU control panel.

4. Your new theme should be visible on the BuddyPress-powered pages of your site.

What just happened?

You may have noticed that the process for installing a theme is very similar to the way WordPress MU handles themes. However, in the case of BuddyPress, you are setting the theme globally for your users.

If you would like to have the BuddyPress theme appear as the theme for your home page, you need to move the bphome theme from `/wp-content/bp-themes/bphome` to `/wp-content/themes/bphome` and enable it the way you would enable a normal WordPress MU theme.

Have a go hero – designing your own theme

BuddyPress comes with a skeleton theme that you can use to build your own theme files. You can find the skeleton theme in your `/wp-content/bp-themes` folder.

The skeleton theme comes with all the template files you will need, as well as some sample CSS files. The skeleton theme's CSS is divided into several files—`base.css`, `activity.css`, `blogs.css`, `directories.css`, `friends.css`, `groups.css`, `messages.css`, `profile.css`, and `wire.css`. Each file is responsible for its own section of the site.

Creating a BuddyPress theme that has a similar look and feel to a WordPress MU theme requires a decent knowledge of CSS and HTML. But the skeleton file is very clear and well organized, which makes the job a lot easier.

Putting BuddyPress content on your front page

The BuddyPress suite comes with several useful widgets that you can use to promote the social network side of your site. These include a Who's Online widget that shows the avatars or gravatars of the users that are online; a Sitewide Activity widget that works like a sitewide Wire, showing recent posts, comments, and group activity; and a Groups widget that shows a selection of the groups available on the site.

To enable the widgets, just go to **Appearance | Widgets** in your WordPress MU admin panel. Add the widgets you wish to use to the sidebar in which you would like them to appear.

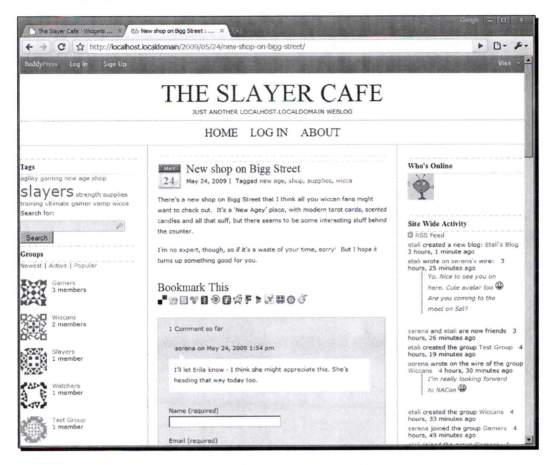

Hooking up BuddyPress to other social networks

BuddyPress is still a relatively new system, but there are already plugins available to work with Twitter and Facebook. There are other plugins currently in development, including one for the OpenID system, which will allow users to log in to any OpenID powered site with just one username and password.

Time for action – Facebook Connect

1. Download the BB-FBConnect plugin from
    `http://wordpress.org/extend/plugins/bp-fbconnect/`.

2. Upload the plugin to your `/wp-content/plugins` folder and enable it as normal.

3. Go to **Settings | Facebook Connect** and click on the link to request a Facebook
    API key.

4. You will need to be a registered Facebook user. Log in to your Facebook account,
    give the application a title (the name of your web site will do), read and accept
    the terms of service, and request an API key. This plugin works with Facebook
    Connect. The current version (1.1) supports only logging in, but the developer
    hopes to add friends list and status update support in the near future.

5. Make a note of the API key and the Secret key at the top of the page.

6. Fill out the basic information about your application. You can edit these details later,
    so if you don't yet have a logo or a privacy policy set up, don't worry too much.

7. On the **Connect** tab, be sure to enter the base URL of your blog in the **Connect
    URL** field; otherwise, Facebook will not accept connections from the remote site.

8. Go back to your admin panel and paste the code Facebook gave you into the
    BB-FBConnect plugin setup page.

9. If the **Connect With Facebook** button does not appear, you may need to add the
    following code to your theme file in the location you want the login link to be:

    ```php
    <?php do_action('fbc_display_login_button') ?>
    ```

10. When the user clicks on the **Connect With Facebook** button, a Facebook login
    window should appear asking them to sign in.

What just happened?

The Facebook Connect plugin uses the Facebook API to allow you to tie your site in to
Facebook. At the moment, the plugin supports only logging in, but this is still useful to your
users, as it saves them from having to manage login details for yet another site.

The Facebook API has many other features, and newer versions of the plugin should offer
even more useful functions such as the ability to update both your blog network's status
feed and your Facebook feed at the same time.

If your sign-in box does not work immediately, double-check that you have filled in everything correctly on the Facebook Developers site. If everything looks fine, wait a while—it can sometimes take a few minutes for changes made on Facebook's end to propagate across all the servers Facebook is using.

Integrating with Twitter

Twitter is a **microblogging** service that lets you broadcast short messages known as Tweets. People who are following you on the service will be able to see those tweets, along with the people who search Twitter for a keyword that you have mentioned and people who just happen to browse through to your profile.

Twitter started as a small "friends only" service and has rapidly grown to attract businesses, sports people, and celebrities. To give you an idea of the popularity of the service, even Oprah has sent tweets!

There is a very good Twitter-to-BuddyPress plugin available at `http://wordpress.org/ extend/plugins/twittertowire/installation/`. Install this plugin to your `mu-plugins` folder and individual users can set up their Twitter account details on their settings page in BuddyPress. The tweets can sometimes take a few minutes to appear.

Improving your site's performance

WordPress MU and BuddyPress can be quite demanding on your server. For this reason, it is a good idea to use some form of caching system. Other performance enhancing techniques will be discussed in depth in the next chapter, but for now, let's turn on object caching.

Time for action – speeding up BuddyPress

1. Open your `wp-config.php` file.

2. Add the following line to it (after lines of code about the database is a good place):

   ```
   define ('WP_CACHE', true);
   ```

3. Download one of the caching systems available at `http://neosmart.net/dl.php?id=14`. If you don't know which one you need, just download the basic file-based version.

4. Upload the files to the `/wp-content/` folder.

5. Now you're good to go. Make sure everything works as normal. In day-to-day use you shouldn't see much of a change in speed, but once you get a lot of users, it will make a big difference.

What just happened?

Your WordPress MU and BuddyPress sites now use a cache to reduce server load. The cache is used as a way to store frequently accessed data in an easy-to-read file instead of in the database. This means that when a lot of people request the same page at the same time, instead of having to make lots of connections to the database, read out what it needs, and process lots of PHP code, the server can just send over a prebuilt version of the page to everyone who wants it. This is faster and more efficient, enabling your site to cope with much higher amounts of traffic.

There are some downsides to caching. It takes up some disk space and, if the page changes, the cached version of it will need to be regenerated. But the caching system that WordPress MU uses is very efficient at dealing with these issues, and you should find that it runs well on your site.

Pop quiz – so many things BuddyPress can do

1. Which of the following is not a default feature of BuddyPress?

   a) Groups.

   b) The Wire—similar to Facebook's Wall.

   c) Friends lists.

   d) Auctions—selling things eBay style.

2. Which of the following is a downside of the BuddyPress caching system?

   a) It eats memory.

   b) It eats disk space.

   c) It drinks blood.

   d) If a page is changed, it will need to be regenerated.

Answers: (1) d, (2) b and d [If (c) were a downside, the Slayers would stake the server!]

The future of BuddyPress

BuddyPress is still a relatively new plugin suite. It currently offers webmasters the ability to run a highly functional social networking site. However, there are some features that are still missing, including privacy options (ideal for the Slayers, who don't want their Watchers spying on their every move), a photo-sharing feature, and closer integration with other social networking sites. The good news is that all of these features are currently being worked on and BuddyPress is advancing quite rapidly.

The best place to learn more about BuddyPress is on the `BuddyPress.org` web site. The community on there is very helpful and the documentation in the codex covers most common questions. You can also download the latest builds of BuddyPress from the trunk, although you should use those builds on a testing server only, and not in a production environment!

Summary

In this chapter we covered the BuddyPress plugin suite. This suite has a lot of powerful social networking features and integrates well with WordPress MU. Your users could spend all their time on the "social" side of your site if they want, and they would still be able to enjoy the blogs, forum posts, and other contributions made by their fellow users.

It is up to each individual webmaster to decide if he/she would prefer to have the emphasis on the blogging side or on the community side of their site.

Specifically, we learned how to install BuddyPress and how to integrate BuddyPress with bbPress and WordPress MU so that you have a fully featured social network and blogging site, rather than something that feels like three different web sites.

We learned about the different features of BuddyPress, including groups, user feeds, and the wire, and we talked about how you can promote the most interesting groups and the most active users.

We learned how to change the theme of your BuddyPress site—either by altering an existing one or by making your own. We also learned how to allow your users to bring in updates from other popular social services such as Facebook Connect and Twitter.

Finally, we learned about using a caching system to reduce the load BuddyPress produces on the server. We also discussed some of the features that the BuddyPress developers are planning for future versions and how to stay up to date on future developments.

Now that we've got the social side of our site up and running, it's time to look at ways to monetize our site so that we can pay the hosting bills and hopefully make a profit!

10
Monetizing Your Site

WordPress MU-and BuddyPress-powered sites require fairly powerful hosting when compared to a single-user blog. If you are running a blog network for use by the general public, rather than a blog for an existing group such as a club or company, you will need to find some way to recoup the server costs. Fortunately, WordPress MU and BuddyPress lend themselves to monetization by a number of different methods.

In this chapter we shall:

- Learn about some of the different monetization options available to us
- Learn how to manage banner ads on your site
- Set up a simple premium membership feature
- Set up revenue sharing

So let's get on with it...

Ways to monetize your site

There are several ways that you can monetize a popular web site. The methods you choose will depend on how popular your site is, the demographics of your visitors, and the nature of the services your site provides. For example, a low traffic site may not make much money from selling banner advertisements; however, if that same site offers access to information that is not easily available elsewhere on the Web, then the users of the site may be willing to pay a subscription fee.

The most common ways of making money from web sites include:

- Advertising networks (CPA/CPM)
- Selling ads directly
- Revenue sharing
- Selling products related to the site's niche
- Membership fees for premium features

The above list is not exhaustive, but it should give you an idea of the options open to you.

In this chapter we will learn how the above monetization methods work. First we will talk about ways to make money with advertising, and then we will consider some other options that involve premium memberships and selling extra services to our members. These options may be preferable if you feel that your users may be put off by advertisements or find them intrusive.

We will also learn how to implement these solutions.

Advertising networks as a revenue source

If you've ever tried to sell advertising space on a web site, then you may have encountered terms such as CPM, CPC, and CPA. **CPM** stands for **Cost Per Thousand** (where M is the letter used to represent 1000 in Roman numerals), **CPC** stands for **Cost Per Click**, and **CPA** stands for **Cost Per Action**.

CPM advertising is useful for high volume sites, although most advertisers set a limit on the number of times they will pay for a particular visitor to view their advertisement per day. This means CPM is not always suitable for sites that generate a large number of page views per visitor—such as forums and social networking communities. Of course, you can negate this issue if you have several advertisers by setting up your ad software to ensure that it rotates the ads that it shows to each visitor.

CPC and CPA advertising can be very profitable in some niches, but you will need to find advertisements that interest your users so that they click on them (for CPC) and sign up or purchase (for CPA).

Google AdSense is a very popular example of CPC advertising. It is also one of the easiest for new publishers to join. Google AdSense reads the content of your page and displays ads that it thinks are related to that content. How relevant those ads are can vary, but webmasters can preview the ads it selects and block advertisements they don't want to appear. The rate of pay offered by advertisers can vary, but there are almost always ads available, so it is a useful program to join.

For the best results, you should look into specialist advertising companies. Some good general ones include Value Click Media, Ad|Media, and Burst Media. There are many other companies, including some that specialize in particular niches such as video games or men's/women's interest topics. You should find that you get better rates from joining an advertising network related to your site's niche.

Selling ads directly

Selling advertisements directly can be a very good solution for some sites. However, before you attempt it, you should make sure that the terms of any advertising networks you are a member of do not prohibit you from doing so.

The main benefits of selling advertising directly are that you can charge a higher rate, you don't lose a cut of the payments to a third party, and you can communicate with the advertiser to get banners that match your site or negotiate for more unusual deals. For example, you could run a "site takeover" where your site's branding is converted to promote a specific product, and you run competitions for your members that are sponsored by the company buying the advertising.

This kind of arrangement can be very beneficial to all parties. For example, SlayerCafe could partner with a combat supplies company that sells crossbows, stakes, and hand-to-hand fighting weapons. The administrator's blog could run a series of reviews covering products sold by the combat supplies company and run competitions with prizes provided by the company. This means the combat supplies store gets advertisements on a site that is read by people who are actually interested in its products; SlayerCafe gets paid well to place relevant advertisements and offer content that its readers are interested in, and the readers get to enjoy quality, relevant content instead of flashing banner ads inviting them to punch a monkey to win $1000.

Unless you are a very popular site, you may find it hard to fill all of your ad spaces through direct sales. It is a good idea to have some other form of advertising to fall back on to fill any empty spaces.

Link sales

Another popular monetization method is selling links. Many webmasters buy links on popular web sites in the hopes of increasing their Google Page Rank. If you plan on selling links, you should consider how Google will view this. Selling links for traffic is considered fine (add the "nofollow" tag to the link so that search engines do not consider it), but selling links to increase the buyer's Page Rank is frowned upon by Google and may adversely affect your Page Rank. If you want to keep your Page Rank high (some advertisers use Page Rank as a measure of popularity), then you should think carefully before selling any links.

Selling related products via affiliate marketing can be a good way to make money from your site, while still adding value for your members. SlayerCafe could sell stakes, magic books, crucifixes, holy water, and other slaying-related equipment. If you go down this route with your site, make sure you affiliate with a site only if you would use the products yourself. Promoting bad products will rapidly make your members lose faith in your site.

If you plan to start selling advertisements directly, the best place to start is with a simple **Advertise on this Site** link, either occupying a very small ad block (don't leave a big one empty because it may make potential advertisers question why it has not been filled) or a link in the footer. On the **Advertise on this Site** page, offer some information about your blog network, along with an explanation of why people would want to advertise with you. You can put this information on the page or in a downloadable document called a **Rate Card**.

Your Rate Card should include some traffic and demographic information (how many users and visitors you have and who your target audience is) and some rates for different kinds of ads (either on a monthly basis or per impression/click). If you aren't sure what to charge, look at some other sites within your niche to get an idea of the advertising budgets your customers may have.

Ads in RSS feeds

If you have a lot of RSS feed subscribers, you could use the FeedBurner advertising system to put ads into your feed. You should think carefully before you do this because the average web user is accustomed to seeing ads on web pages and in emails, but RSS feeds are often used on mobile devices, and your readers may feel that ads in an RSS feed are too intrusive and waste their time and bandwidth. Many people still pay per MB on their mobile data packages, so if they feel the content of your feed is not adding value, they will unsubscribe.

Donate links

Asking for donations can work very well on an open source software project site or a web comic. It also works well for charities and non-profit organizations. If your site falls into any of those categories, then you may find that your users are willing to donate money to help keep the site going. However, if you are aiming for a professional image, then having a donation button on your site would detract from that.

Revenue sharing

Revenue sharing is an increasingly popular way of making money from web communities. Revenue sharing sites usually work by giving users a percentage of any revenue generated by ads displayed on any pages containing content the user has created. Some sites pay the users out of their own pocket, but an easier method is to offer an option on the user's profile page for them to add their Google AdSense details and to use those details for a percentage of the ads displayed.

Some well-known revenue sharing sites include the Digital Point webmaster's forums (`http://forums.digitalpoint.com`), the TagTooga Tag Directory (`http://www.tagtooga.com/db.tag`), and the Travel Blog Network "My Life of Travel" (`http://www.mylifeoftravel.com/`).

Usually, revenue sharing sites display their own ads for a certain percentage of page views and then use users' ads for the rest of the page views the site generates. On a blog site, a user's ads have a chance of displaying on their own blog posts. On a forum, a user's ads may be displayed when a thread that they have created is viewed.

Revenue sharing encourages users to contribute and to promote the site. After all, if they don't make any blog posts, they won't make any money. This can be a good thing, as you have lots of people working to promote your site for a comparatively low cost.

The downside of revenue sharing is that it can drive down the quality of contributions. This is especially true on forums. If a user knows that their ads are displayed only if they create a new thread, they may decide to make dozens of spam threads or may start a new thread if they have any question to ask rather than searching forums to see if the question has already been answered in another thread.

If you decide to use revenue sharing, you should make sure that you have good moderation processes in place to avoid spammers trying to exploit the system. Revenue sharing can be an effective method of encouraging contributors and getting members to promote your site. The administrative burden of keeping the site free of spam could be a problem if you have a small team of moderators; however, if you have the time to invest, you may find that the promotion and "free" content your users generate is worth the effort.

Often, some simple measures such as requiring a certain number of posts or members to be active for a certain period of time before they gain access to the revenue sharing benefits of the site are sufficient to keep the quality of your users' blog and forum posts high.

Premium memberships

If your site offers a service that cannot easily be obtained elsewhere, then you are in a good position to offer premium memberships. Most people expect to be able to enjoy access to web sites without paying a fee, so it is a good idea to leave at least the basic features of your site open to all; however, offering extra features to paying members can be a good way to make money from your site.

A good starting point is to offer premium members simple upgrades such as the ability to view the site without any banner ads being displayed, more storage space for PMs or images, or the ability to edit their themes in more depth. You could also offer "site supporter" graphics or special ranks for users who have paid for a premium membership, setting them apart from non-paying members of the community and allowing them to show their loyalty to the site.

If you are planning to offer extra storage quotas, you should make sure that your server has sufficient space to allow you to offer that benefit. Also, if you are allowing users to edit their themes, you should set that up in such a way that the themes can be moderated to make sure that they do not contain any malicious code.

Selling products via your site

There are a number of ways you can sell products via your site. Going back to the combat store example, an affiliate store could work well. Affiliate offerings such as the Amazon Store aren't as popular as they were a few years ago, but there are still people who have stores that are performing well. The best results come from well-designed stores that offer products related to their niche.

Many communities offer t-shirts, caps, bags, and other items through printing companies such as CafePress (`http://www.cafepress.com/`) or SpreadShirt (`http://www.spreadshirt.co.uk/`). Those companies allow you to create clothes and other items with your own designs on them and then set the price of those items. They set a base price and anything you charge above that price is given to you. T-shirts and similar items are, in my experience, most popular with sites that are based around a fairly tight-knit community. If your community members enjoy having real-life meets from time to time, you may see a spike in t-shirt sales around the time of the meet.

Another option available for selling is books. Companies such as Lulu (`http://www.Lulu.com`) allow you to make your own booklets. Their prices are much higher than a traditional publisher's, but you can produce any book you want. This means that a Watcher could produce a niche booklet called *Zen and the Art of Slaying*, which no normal publisher would even consider (as they probably think that Vampires don't even exist!), and sell it to Slayers around the world. You could also offer parts of the book as a digital download, either for free as a form of promotion or as a discounted product to drive extra sales.

Managing ads on WordPress MU

Now that you know a little about some of the more common ways of monetizing a site, let's get started with one of the simplest options—advertising.

If you're planning on using only one advertiser and aren't expecting to need to move your ads around very much, you could hardcode your ads into the themes you're using on your site. However, this isn't ideal. It means that every time you decide to change advertisers, you'd have to edit your theme files. It also makes it very difficult to set up any form of rotation to handle multiple ads.

Using an ad management plugin makes life a lot easier.

Time for action – ad management with Advertising Manager

Let's start by setting up an ad management plugin for WordPress MU:

1. Download the Advertising Manager plugin from `http://wordpress.org/extend/plugins/advertising-manager/screenshots/` and install to your `mu-plugins` folder.

2. Go to the **Ads** section of your admin panel and select **Create New**.

3. Paste in the ad code for the advertisement you'd like to display. (I've used a Google banner ad, which will go in the footer of the blog.)

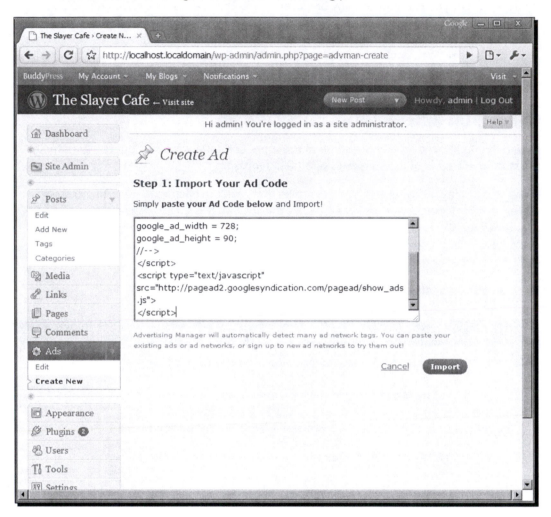

4. Click **Import**. Advertising Manager should read the details of the ad and display an options page where you can set up some more detailed options relating to the ad.

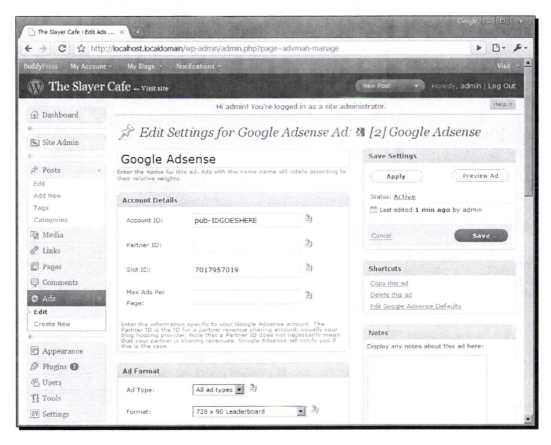

5. The default options are fine for now, so just change the Google AdSense name to something shorter but still descriptive (I chose "google"), and save the ad.

6. To add the advertisement to your theme, open the theme file and paste the following code where you would like the advertisement to appear:

```php
<?php advman_ad('google'); ?>
```

7. If you need to add more advertisements, just replace "google" with the name you would like to use for the other ad.

What just happened?

Advertising Manager is an easy-to-use advertising solution for WordPress MU. If you wish to display ads on certain kinds of pages across the entire blog network, then Advertising Manager is the plugin to use.

It works with all kinds of ads; just paste the ad code in, set a few options, and you're good to go.

When you're managing multiple ads, the more advanced features will allow you to dictate the kinds of pages that the ad appears on (so that you can have different ads on a category page as compared to the ones that appear on a page with a single post, for example) and to change the "weight" of an ad. This means you can make sure that the most important advertisements are prioritized so that you can fill your impressions quota for them. Just give the most important ads a higher weight value than the less important ones.

One useful feature of Advertising Manager is its support for OpenX Market. You can configure Advertising Manager to look at the available advertisements on the OpenX Market and, if the CPM for one of those advertisements is higher than the value you have set on the Settings screen, Advertising Manager will display the OpenX ad instead of one of your normal ads. All it takes is a couple of clicks in the **Settings | Ads** screen to configure OpenX Market optimization.

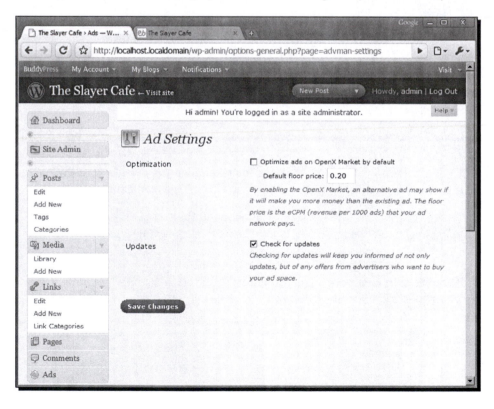

Have a go hero - advertising

When it comes to advertising, the trick is to find places to put your advertisements that will attract the attention of your visitors without annoying them.

The best place to put an advertisement will vary from site to site, but it is generally accepted that you should try to place your most important advertisements "above the fold" so that the user sees them without scrolling down.

Many people also place advertisements in sidebars, but I believe that those ads are likely to be overlooked. This is because people who spend a lot of time on the web tend to become "ad blind" and are able to tune out ads and see only the content they are looking for.

You can put ads near your navigation. (But don't blend them such that they look like real navigation links, as users hate this and it could be against the terms of service of your advertisers.) In that case those ads could perform well. Also, try placing ads in between content sections.

Spend some time tweaking your layout and deciding where you would like to place some ads. Remember that the code to add to your templates to display the ads should look something like:

```php
<?php advman_ad('ADNAME'); ?>
```

You can give the same name to multiple ads. If you do this, those ads will be rotated according to their weight.

The ad template tags should work in bbPress.

Revenue sharing

Giving your users a chance to get something back for their contributions to the site is a nice way to encourage participation in the community and hopefully get your users to promote the site to their friends. Setting up revenue sharing is relatively easy—thanks to a plugin from Elad Salomons.

Time for action – revenue sharing

1. Download the AdSense revenue sharing plugin from `http://wpmudev.org/ project/adsense-revenue-sharing/installation` and install it.

2. Go to **Site Admin | AdSense share**, add your AdSense publisher code, and set the percentage of ad views you wish to share. SlayerCafe has chosen to share 50 percent of the generated impressions.

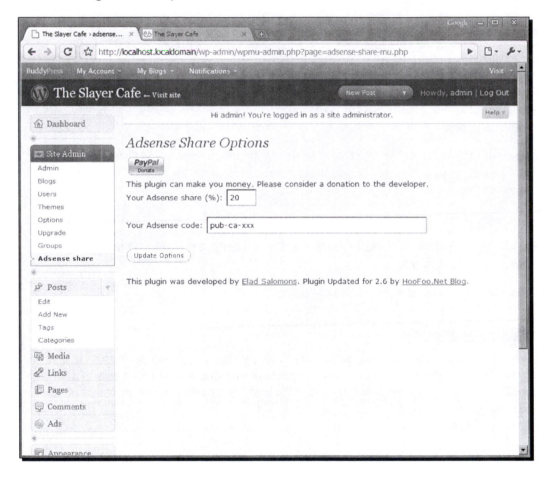

3. Your users can add their own publisher ID via the **Settings | AdSense Publisher** menu.

What just happened?

We now have a simple revenue sharing system in place. If one of our users wants to join the revenue sharing, they can add their personal Google AdSense code in the admin panel. When a visitor comes to that user's blog, there is a 50 percent chance that they will see an advertisement that uses SlayerCafe's Google AdSense code and a 50 percent chance that they will see an advertisement tied to the AdSense account of the user who created the blog.

A revenue sharing system like this should encourage your users to post regular updates on their blog, and to promote their blog—the more page views they receive, the more times their advertisements will be shown, and the more money they will earn.

Premium memberships

Premium memberships are a good way to offer extra value-added services. There are several options for setting up premium memberships for WordPress MU. The best option for your site will depend on your budget, the features you want to make use of, and the amount of time you are willing to spend tweaking your site to set up the premium features.

If you are after a solution that works out of the box and is familiar to a large number of your users, then the WPMU DEV Upgrades plugin is a good premium solution. You can find out more about it at `http://premium.wpmudev.org/project/upgrades`.

Joining WPMU DEV costs $79 for a month's worth of access. For that fee you get access to all of their premium plugins, which can be reused and modified under the rules of the GPL. The membership fee may seem expensive, but it is worth for the support they offer and the wealth of premium plugins.

The WPMU DEV Upgrades plugin allows you to offer to your users "upgrades", which they can purchase under a credits system, much like the system used by WORDPRESS.COM.

If you are looking for a free solution, there are several options open to you, but they will require more backend work to get up and running than the WPMU DEV plugins.

MemberWing

The MemberWing Membership plugin is available in both free and premium versions. You can download it from `http://www.memberwing.com/`. It requires the IonCube Loader to be installed on your server. The free version has most of the features of the paid one (such as multiple levels of membership and teaser pages), but members must be manually added and removed from the list of subscribers. Also, the free version is branded and subscribers-only pages have links back to MemberWing.com. This makes it less attractive for use on a production site; however, if you are considering purchasing the paid version, then the free version is worthwhile as a trial.

EasyPaypal

EasyPaypal is a WordPress plugin that also works with WordPress MU. You can download it from `http://www.codeplex.com/easypaypal/Release/ProjectReleases.aspx?ReleaseId=13663`. This plugin allows you to hide specific content or posts from non-paying members and restrict certain functions such as publishing posts. We will be using EasyPaypal in our example setup.

Time for action – premium memberships

1. Install EasyPaypal on your main blog. If you want to restrict functions on user blogs, use **Plugin Commander** to force it to be active for all users.

2. Go to **Settings | EasyPaypal Configuration** to set up your payment options. It is a good idea to use the Paypal sandbox to test everything first.

The Slayer Cafe › EasyPay...   The Slayer Cafe

http://localhost.localdomain/wp-admin/options-general.php?page=easypaypal/easypaypal_

BuddyPress   My Account ▾   My Blogs ▾   Notifications ▾   Visit ▾

The Slayer Cafe ← Visit site   New Post ▾   Howdy, admin | Log Out

Hi admin! You're logged in as a site administrator.   Help ▾

🏠 Dashboard

📑 Site Admin

EasyPayPal Configuration

Configure EasyPalPal below. For help, see the support page

» User Manager

📌 Posts
  Edit
  Add New
  Tags
  Categories

☑ Use PayPal Sandbox (testing only)

To disable login subscriptions, enter 9999 in the **Trial Period** below.

🖼 Media
  Library
  Add New

| Authorization Code | slayersftw123 | Enter a unique code here. It will be combined with today's date and encrypted to deter evil PayPal impersonators. Example: PH8675309 |

🔗 Links
  Edit
  Add New
  Link Categories

| Your PayPal Email Address | myemail@domain.com | The email address through which you will receive payments. |
| Item Name | SlayerCafe Supporter | The name of the item or service to display on the PayPal order form. |

📄 Pages

💬 Comments

| Item Number | 1 | A number, defined by you, to represent this item for tracking purposes. |
| Payment Amount | 5 | The payment amount per period. Example: 45.00 |

🔘 Ads

| Currency Code | USD | The currency code for the payment amount. Example: USD |

🖼 Appearance
🔌 Plugins ❷
👥 Users

| Payment Period (days) | 90 | The number of days between payments. Example: 30 |

🔧 Tools

| Trial Period (days) | 0 | The number of days for a trial period. Blank or zero for no trial. Enter 9999 to turn off subscriptions completely. |

⚙ Settings

---

3. As Slayers aren't usually rich people (fighting evil every night makes it difficult to hold down a day job), the subscription fee has been set at a low rate—$5 for 90 days.

4. Further down the configuration page, there is an option to set restricted categories. Let's make two categories—Special Operations and Supporters. These will only be accessible to members with a current subscription.

5. In the **Login Message** box, you can add some subscription code. This takes the name of the product, the product number, the cost, currency code, and the number of days the subscription is valid for. See the following for an example:

```
[paybutton]{Supporters}|{1}|{5}|{USD}|{90}|{Hidden Text}[/
paybutton]
```

6. Now, when a user tries to view a subscriber's only post, they should see a message like this:

What just happened?

We have created a basic premium membership service using a free WordPress MU plugin. This allows us to lock down certain features of the site to those who are premium members. The EasyPaypal site allows us to hide specific categories and posts, and it allows us to prevent users from being able to post certain blogs if they are not members. It is possible to set different membership levels (with different prices), so we can offer subscriptions appropriate to the needs and wallets of our members.

On SlayerCafe that means:

◆ Official Slayer: A discounted full membership. Being a Slayer is difficult, and not all Slayers are able to hold down full-time jobs, so paying an expensive membership fee is not an option. Slayers can see all the premium content on the site.

◆ Official Watcher: Watchers tend to be older than Slayers and have more money. They also need some features which Slayers would not be interested in, such as the ability to upload large PDF scans of ancient documents.

◆ SlayerCafe Angel: We have referred to our mystical friends (Wiccans, good Werewolves, and Vampires that have souls) as Angels. Members in this category have access to most features of the site, but there is some content that they are not allowed to see.

◆ SlayerCafe Supporter: This category is aimed at people who are not directly involved in the fight against vampires. Supporters are given a special title and a special user graphic, and there are some offers and downloads which are only for premium members (which includes supporters). This membership deal allows members of the public to help the site and its members at a low cost.

Of course, before anyone is added to an official category, they will need to be screened by an administrator to confirm their identity.

On SlayerCafe, we do not want to lock down the site to quite that extent, but the site will make use of the Subscribers Only categories in order to inform paying members of special offers and keep them up to date with exclusive news postings.

You can use the EasyPaypal plugin in conjunction with the Role Manager plugin to give users who donate (or subscribe) extra benefits. You could manage this either by setting the user's role manually when they pay or by using the following code in `easypaypal_return.php`— add it inside the `if($epp_days_to_add > 0)` statement.

```
$user = new WP_User($user_ID)
$user->set_role("subscriber")
```

The above code will set paid users to subscribers and will make sure that the subscriber role has the permissions you want to give to paying members.

As the permissions given to users on SlayerCafe simply involve displaying a different graphic to indicate that they have donated money to the site at some point in the past, we will not be demoting users once their paid period has elapsed. If you wish to demote users, you can do so by adding some similar code to the function, which checks if a user's subscription has expired.

If your community is relatively small, you may find that promoting and demoting members manually works for you, as this gives you more control over the privileges you give each member and you can tailor benefits for each person.

Have a go hero – hiding ads from paid members

One premium feature that many users would enjoy is the ability to surf without ads.

In an earlier chapter, we learned how to display certain menu options to users who are not logged in. Try using what we learned there to alter our themes so that advertisements are displayed only to users who are either not logged in or do not have the role of subscriber.

Other ways to monetize your site—stores

Earlier in the chapter, we touched on using services such as CafePress to monetize your site. If you would like to sell merchandise on your store, then CafePress combined with the Wishads For CafePress Store plugin is an easy way to get started. There are similar plugins for other services. I am highlighting this one simply because it is attractive and easy to use. All you need to do is install your plugin, enter your CafePress API details, and you're ready to go.

You will need an account with `CafePress.com` to use the plugin. You can download the plugin from `http://wordpress.org/extend/plugins/wishads-for-cafepress-store/`.

At the time of writing, Wishads for CafePress Stores does not work with WordPress MU 2.8.4; however, the author is working on updating the plugin. You can see a demo of the store at `http://wishads.com/wordpress_2_6_2`.

The plugin is ideal for selling merchandise ranging from t-shirts to bumper stickers, flasks, and even mini video cameras, all with your branding on it. So, if a version of the plugin is released that is suitable for your version of WordPress MU, I highly recommend that you try it out.

Things to remember when monetizing your site

When you are considering how to monetize your site, try to think about how your site will appear from the point of view of the users. The chances are that as a user, you don't enjoy sites with large amounts of advertisements. You may also be turned off by sites that constantly promote merchandise or try to get you to pay for features.

In the early days of building a community, it is important to encourage members to be active and to promote the site to their friends. As your traffic grows, you can start offering paid-for upgrades, subscriptions, and ad-free surfing.

If you plan to make a feature premium, make sure that it's something that would be "nice to have", but isn't essential to using the site. One example would be RSS feeds. Some sites allow anyone to visit and browse through the site's latest additions but offer RSS only to premium members.

Summary

In this chapter we talked about ways to make money from your site.

We learned about advertising, including a look at some of the most important terminology (such as CPC, CPA, and CPM) and how to manage multiple advertising campaigns on your web site. We also covered revenue sharing and how it can encourage your users to be more active on the web site. We talked about the problems that revenue sharing can cause and how to combat them.

We learned how to offer paid subscriptions with different privileges for different user levels, and we also talked about other ways to make money from your site with affiliate programs, merchandise, and donations.

We also talked about things that you should remember when trying to make money from a web community so that your money-making attempts do not frustrate or drive away your visitors.

Now that we've got some ideas for how to monetize our user base, let's make sure that our server can handle all those users! The next chapter will cover optimizing the site so that it can cope with large amounts of traffic.

11
Site Optimization

With the exception of small personal home pages, almost every webmaster wants to see their site take off. However, the unfortunate thing about the Web is the price associated in the form of server load and bandwidth usage with the high volumes of traffic. If you want your site to run well during times of high traffic, you'll need to optimize it as much as possible.

In this chapter, we will learn about:

- Caching systems—a simple but effective way of reducing server load
- Optimizing your database files in order to keep things running smoothly
- Speeding up loading times for your users by optimizing theme files
- Techniques for troubleshooting slow loading times

So let's get started...

Choosing to optimize your site

WordPress MU is a resource-hungry web application. This isn't a reflection on the people who have worked on it or the quality of the code, rather it is more of a side effect of how powerful WordPress MU is. As an administrator of a WordPress MU-powered site, you are giving your users the ability to run their own web sites—something that was pretty difficult for an individual to do even just a few years ago.

You can set up your site and test it on a good shared hosting package. But if you get more than a few users, you'll quickly hit the limits of what a shared host will allow you to do. Really, to run a WordPress MU site that will get more than a handful of visitors, you need a VPS or, ideally, a dedicated server.

Shared hosting packages are relatively inexpensive; however, the low cost is offset by the fact that your site is located on the same physical server as hundreds of other sites. If any of the sites on the server use an excessive amount of resources, then all of the sites on that server could suffer from instability and slow loading times.

A **VPS** is a **Virtual Private Server**. You rent a virtual computer, which you can set up any way you like, and you have a lot more control over how the server is run. Your server runs on the same hardware as several other VPSes but, in general, companies do not "oversell" VPS packages, so you should not be fighting for resources as much as you would be on a shared package.

Another option is a dedicated server, which gives you full control over all the hardware. This is the most expensive option, but it is a good idea for very large sites.

For most people, a VPS is a good starting point—they're inexpensive, offer you a lot of flexibility, and can grow with you. The fact that you have root access to a VPS makes life a lot easier when it comes to changing server settings. Also, if your site takes off, you should be able to make the move to a dedicated server fairly easily.

Most VPS accounts offer large amounts of hard drive space, but they have comparatively small memory limits and data transfer limits. These limitations would not be an issue for, say, a web designer offering their clients static "Business card on the web" style sites, but a social networking and blogging site is likely to hit the limits of a smaller VPS account pretty quickly.

Going over your data transfer limit can be quite costly. You could end up with a large bill for the extra bandwidth usage (many hosts charge a per GB fee for excess usage, and some less reputable hosts even charge per MB!), or your site could be taken offline by your web hosting provider until the end of the month. When buying your hosting, make sure you check the terms and conditions so that you don't get any nasty surprises.

Most VPS services allow you to burst over the normal memory limitations on your account for short periods of time, but if your site is running at a higher load than the server can cope with for extended periods, then they may disable your account or limit it in some way, leaving you with a slow and possibly not a fully functional site.

The above are just some of the problems you could encounter with an unoptimized site. Fortunately, making your site load more quickly and consume fewer resources is not difficult.

Speed up your site with caching

Adding a cache is the easiest way to speed up your site. It's simple to set up and has very little impact on what your visitors see (except for, hopefully, faster page loading times).

WordPress developer Donncha made a very powerful caching plugin called WP Super Cache. At the time of writing, this plugin worked only for versions of WordPress MU up to 2.7.1; however, it is worth checking the plugin's page to see if it has been updated to work with WordPress MU 2.8. You can find out more about the plugin at `http://wordpress.org/extend/plugins/wp-super-cache/`.

For the moment, Donncha has made a simple object cache for newer versions of WordPress MU.

Time for action – setting up object cache

The object cache system uses just one file, which means that it is simple to set up:

1. Download the file from `http://ocaoimh.ie/wp-content/uploads/2009/05/object-cache.txt`.

2. Rename the file to `object-cache.php` and upload it to your `/wp-content` folder. Note that this is not a plugin, so it doesn't need to go in the `plugins` folder.

3. The cache should start working immediately. View a post on your site and then check `/wp-content/cache`.

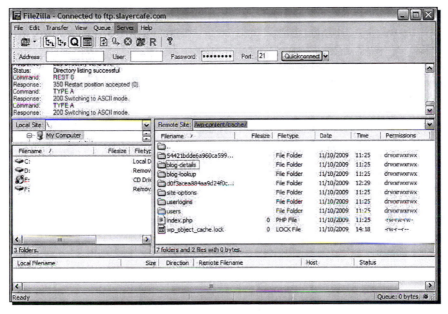

4. If there's nothing in that folder, check the file permissions. Setting them to 755 via your FTP client (or using `chmod` if you prefer to use the shell) should be sufficient for most server setups.

5. Once files start appearing in the `/wp-content/cache` folder, you can be confident the cache is working.

What just happened?

Donncha's object cache isn't exactly flashy, but it gets the job done. The cache is still experimental, but in the testing I've done, I have found that it works well. Donncha offers some more information about the cache on his site

`http://ocaoimh.ie/looking-at-a-wpmu-object-cache/.`

Caching works by saving frequently used pages, either to memory or to the hard drive. If you don't have a cache when a page is viewed, the web server has to read the PHP code and interpret it to "build" the page. For a WordPress MU site with BuddyPress and bbPress installed, that could mean several database queries need to be completed to put the page together. If a typical page shows a list of logged in users, recent comments, recent posts, popular blog posts, and the content of a blog post, then the database will need to be queried at least once for each of those things.

If one of your users writes an incredibly interesting or amusing article that makes it to the front page of a social bookmarking site, you could have hundreds of visitors all trying to view the same page at once. This means your server would have to do the same queries over and over for every single visitor.

It's much faster to display a static HTML file than it is to display a page that needs several database queries to put it together. It's for this reason that caching is useful. The first time the page is viewed, a copy of it is made as a static HTML page. This copy is then served up to any future visitors, freeing up those extra database connection slots for more important things.

The downsides of caching and how to avoid them

Cached files take up hard drive space (or memory, if you're not using a filesystem-based cache). Storing information multiple times seems like a waste of time at first, especially if you have hundreds of pages cached at the same time. Fortunately, cached files expire after a while, so you shouldn't find your hard drive space vanishing too quickly. Also, you can always empty the cache manually (just delete all the files in the `/wp-content/cache` folder) if you feel it's getting out of hand.

Also, cached pages are, by their nature, static. This means they can become out of date. If you make some changes to your site, they may not be reflected on any cached pages. Again, you can work around this by clearing your cache after any major changes.

More ways to speed up your site—optimizing themes

If you are expecting a lot of traffic to your blog network, then a caching system alone may not be enough to ensure that all your visitors have a good, speedy experience.

Optimizing your theme files is another simple, low-cost way to speed things up. There are a couple of changes that you can make—some reduce the load your site generates on the server, while others simply speed up the loading time that your users will experience.

Spreading the load

If you expect your site to be extremely popular, you may need to spread the load across multiple servers. A simple way to do so is to move frequently accessed files such as images and CSS files to a separate server. The Amazon S3 service is an inexpensive way to do this.

Amazon's S3 service is a "pay as you go" hosting service for static files. You pay only for what you use—a nominal amount per request and a small amount per GB of traffic, with different charges for uploads and downloads. There's no minimum fee, so the service is useful even for sites with lower amounts of traffic.

Amazon S3 is useful for sites that are coming close to the bandwidth allowances of their normal hosting, as it will often work out cheaper in such cases to pay for what you're using on S3 rather than upgrade your hosting account.

If you don't think that you need separate hosting with S3 for your site just yet, you can still speed up the loading of your page for your visitors by emulating the use of different hosts by placing frequently requested images on different subdomains.

Time for action – spreading the load

1. If you plan on using Amazon S3, sign up for an account at `https://aws-portal.amazon.com/gp/aws/developer/subscription/index.html`.

2. Create a bucket for your files. Pick a unique name such as `assets.mysite`.

3. Using your site's WHM control panel (or edit the DNS Settings file for the site on your VPS), create a CNAME record for this bucket called s3, and point it to `assets.mysite.s3.amazonaws.com.` (the period at the end of this is important).

4. If you aren't planning on using Amazon S3, then instead of using a CNAME record like the one in step 3, just create some subdomains called assets1, assets2, and so on. You can then create those subdomains as VirtualHosts in Apache.

5. Upload popular theme files (your logo, nav buttons, CSS files, and so on) either to Amazon S3 or to those subdomains.

6. Edit your theme files to reflect the change in path to the assets. If you're using different subdomains, you could have images on assets1, JavaScript on assets2, and so on.

That's it, you're good to go.

What just happened?

You are now serving different parts of your site from different servers. If you are using Amazon's S3 service, you have actually removed some of the load from your own servers. Even if you're just using a few different subdomains that are still located on your physical server, your visitors should see a speed improvement.

The reason for this is that most browsers will only download a couple of files from a particular server at any time. If your files are located on different subdomains, the browser sees those subdomains as being different servers and will request files from them. Therefore, if you have ten files spread across five servers, the browser will download them all at the same time, instead of downloading a couple, waiting for them to finish, and then downloading some more. This means the limiting factor to how quickly the page is displayed is the viewer's Internet connection speed.

To the end user (and to search engines), there is no difference in the functionality of your site. Only images and CSS files are loaded from the other servers; the important parts of your site are still located on your main server. All your page addresses remain the same. The only change that your users will notice is that the site loads more quickly.

More theme optimization

Another theme optimization, which can speed up sites that are operating under heavy load is to hardcode as much of the theme's content as possible.

Take a look at the `header.php` file. (I'm using the default header for this example, as it's fairly simple, so the code is clearer.)

```
<!DOCTYPE html PUBLIC "-//W3C//DTD XHTML 1.0 Transitional//EN"
"http://www.w3.org/TR/xhtml1/DTD/xhtml1-transitional.dtd">
<html xmlns="http://www.w3.org/1999/xhtml" <?php language_
attributes(); ?>>
<head profile="http://gmpg.org/xfn/11">
<meta http-equiv="Content-Type" content="<?php bloginfo('html_type');
?>; charset=<?php bloginfo('charset'); ?>" />

<title><?php wp_title('&laquo;', true, 'right'); ?> <?php
bloginfo('name'); ?></title>
<link rel="stylesheet" href="<?php bloginfo('stylesheet_url'); ?>"
type="text/css" media="screen" />
<link rel="alternate" type="application/rss+xml" title="<?php
bloginfo('name'); ?> RSS Feed" href="<?php bloginfo('rss2_url'); ?>"
/>
<link rel="alternate" type="application/atom+xml" title="<?php
bloginfo('name'); ?> Atom Feed" href="<?php bloginfo('atom_url'); ?>"
/>
<link rel="pingback" href="<?php bloginfo('pingback_url'); ?>" />
<style type="text/css" media="screen">
<?php
// Checks to see whether it needs a sidebar or not
if ( !empty($withcomments) && !is_single() ) {
?>
```

```
    #page { background: url("<?php bloginfo('stylesheet_directory');
?>/images/kubrickbg-<?php bloginfo('text_direction'); ?>.jpg") repeat-
y top; border: none; }
<?php } else { // No sidebar ?>
    #page { background: url("<?php bloginfo('stylesheet_directory');
?>/images/kubrickbgwide.jpg") repeat-y top; border: none; }
<?php } ?>
</style>
<?php if ( is_singular() ) wp_enqueue_script( 'comment-reply' ); ?>
<?php wp_head(); ?>
</head>
<body>
<div id="page">
<div id="header">
    <div id="headerimg">
            <h1><a href="<?php echo get_option('home'); ?>/"><?php
bloginfo('name'); ?></a></h1>
            <div class="description"><?php bloginfo('description'); ?></
div>
    </div>
</div>
<hr />
```

In the above file, all instances of PHP code that are being used to determine something that is fairly unlikely to change (for example, the name of the blog or the path to a theme) have been highlighted.

You could remove the PHP code in each instance and hardcode the value in place. So, for SlayerCafe, you would replace `<?php bloginfo('name'); ?>` with The Slayer Cafe, and `<?php echo get_option('home'); ?>` with `http://www.slayercafe.com`. Before you try this, take a backup of the file!

There are many other examples of this. If you look for the part of your theme file where the list of pages (for example, "About Us") is displayed, you will see that WordPress MU uses a function to display those pages. If you're confident that you won't be adding new pages very often, you could remove that function call and instead hardcode links to the pages that you want to have listed.

I'd recommend taking the time to do these edits on your main blog's theme files, as well as the theme files for BuddyPress and bbPress. Only hardcode values that are not likely to change often such as links to the home page, the title of the blog, and so on. If you decide to edit the themes that will be available to your users, only change things such as the HTML type and the paths to the theme files. Remember that there is one theme shared among many users, so you can't hardcode in every user's blog title!

Compressing the images used in your site's themes will save you some bandwidth. Check to make sure that all your images are saved at the size they are used. All too often, designers save a large image in a high resolution (for example, a logo) and use that large image file on their site, setting the image's dimensions so that it appears much smaller. Instead of wasting your bandwidth, and that of your visitor by making them download a file that could be hundreds of kilobytes (or more!) in size, why not make a smaller, lower resolution version of that file for the Web?

Optimizing your database

Optimizing your database is a simple maintenance task that can greatly improve the performance of your site, especially if you have a large number of active users.

Time for action – optimizing your site through phpMyAdmin

1. Log in to phpMyAdmin and select your site's database. Depending on the web host you are using, your phpMyAdmin may be located in /phpMyAdmin or accessible through your web hosting account's admin panel.

2. Scroll down the list of tables and click **Check All**.

3. From the drop-down menu, select **Optimize table**.

4. Once the optimization task is completed, you should see a screen like this:

What just happened?

We have just optimized our database. As the preceding screenshot was taken after the optimization of a fairly new install of SlayerCafe, there wasn't any optimization required, so every row says **Table is already up to date**. On a less fresh install, you are likely to see several rows saying **OK**, indicating that the optimization was successful.

Optimizing a database is a little like defragmenting your hard drive. As a database is used, rows are added to and deleted from tables. When a row is deleted, a blank space is left in its place. MySQL tries to fill that blank space the next time some data needs to be added to the database, but this isn't always possible, especially if the rows are of variable length. The data to be inserted could be longer than the gap left by the last piece of data removed. Over time, the database could end up with lots of empty spaces spread all over the place. The total amount of empty space in the database is known as **overhead**. Optimizing removes the overhead, leading to a smaller and hopefully faster database.

Have a go hero – automate that optimization!

You should optimize your database frequently. Some administrators of high traffic WordPress MU sites have experienced a benefit from optimizing their database every day. In my experience, most moderately trafficked sites don't need to be optimized every day—I've found once a week works well enough.

Even so, logging in to phpMyAdmin once a week could quickly become tedious. Why not automate the optimization process so that you don't have to remember to log on regularly.

You can automate database optimization using a cron job similar to this one:

```
0 0 * * 1 mysqlcheck -Aao –auto-repair -u root -p[password]
```

You can set up this cron job by adding this text to your crontab if you have shell access on your VPS or by using your web site's admin panel (for example, cPanel has a web interface for setting up cron jobs).

A **cron job** is a job that is scheduled to execute periodically. The frequency of execution is determined by the first part of this line, like this:

```
*   *  *  *  *
-   -  -  -  -
|   |  |  |  |
|   |  |  |  +----- day of week (0 - 6) (Sunday=0)
|   |  |  +------- month (1 - 12)
|   |  +--------- day of month (1 - 31)
|   +----------- hour (0 - 23)
+------------- min (0 - 59)
```

So, in our example, we have told the `mysqlcheck` command to run once every Monday. The command will check the database and autorepair any problems it finds.

Troubleshooting slow loading sites

If you have tried all the optimizations in this chapter, but are still not satisfied with the performance of your site, there are a few troubleshooting techniques you can use to identify the bottleneck.

◆ **Check your themes:**

Use the YSlow plugin (`http://developer.yahoo.com/yslow/`) to perform a range of tests on your theme. Do you have very large images or any broken links that are slowing down the loading of your page? If so, fixing these could give you a quick performance boost.

◆ **Check your plugins:**

Running a large number of plugins can slow down your site. Check through your list of plugins and update any that have had new versions released. Also, try disabling plugins one by one to see if any of them are causing the slowdown.

If it does not appear that a specific plugin is causing the problem, check through your plugin list to see if there are any plugins that you are not using or that you no longer need. Removing these should give you a performance boost.

- **Encourage your users to use turbo**:

  If you are getting complaints from some of your users that the site is slow, but you find the speed satisfying, then encourage your users to try using the **Turbo** setting in the top right-hand corner of the admin panel. Turbo uses Google Gears to speed up the user experience. Certain scripts, images, and other files will be stored on the user's computer, which should greatly speed up loading times for them.

- **Troubleshoot with wp-config**:

  Use the `define('SAVEQUERIES', true);` statement in `wp-config.php` to tell WordPress MU to save a list of database queries as they happen. Then add the following to your `footer.php` file of the main blog's theme:

```php
<?php
if (current_user_can('switch_themes')){
    global $wpdb;
    echo "<pre>";
    print_r($wpdb->queries);
    echo "</pre>";
}
?>
```

  This will cause logged in users with the "switch themes" ability to be able to see a list of database queries involved in loading a page. If you see an exceptionally large number of database queries for a specific page, you can either troubleshoot the source code for that page yourself or ask for help on the WordPress forums.

- **Change the PHP memory limit**:

  If you are getting out of memory errors, try upping the PHP memory limit. This determines how much memory a PHP script is allowed to use. You can find this setting in `PHP.ini`. If you do not have access to `PHP.ini` on your web server, you can set the value for this in `wp-config.php` using this definition:

```php
define('WP_MEMORY_LIMIT', '64M');
```

- **Change how PHP runs**:

  PHP can be run in CGI mode or ISAPI mode. In CGI mode, an instance of PHP is loaded for every PHP file requested. In ISAPI mode, there is one instance used for every page. ISAPI mode usually performs better for sites experiencing high load. If you aren't sure how PHP is running on your server, talk to your web host. You may find that changing the PHP mode will improve your site's performance.

Server side optimizations

Optimizing Apache, PHP, and MySQL is beyond the scope of this book, but if you are expecting large amounts of traffic or simply want to squeeze as much power as possible out of your existing server setup, then the topic is worth investigating.

Many webmasters have found that using lighttpd or nginx instead of Apache offers a performance boost. Also, tweaking the settings for MySQL and PHP may help you. If you need advice about how to do this, I would recommend contacting your web host.

Some tweaks are possible only on a VPS hosting plan or better. It is possible to run WordPress MU and BuddyPress on a shared hosting plan; however, if you find yourself hitting the limits of such a plan, the best option is to upgrade to a VPS. If you have difficulty on a smaller VPS plan (for example, 256MB RAM), again an upgrade may be the easiest fix. However, for plans bigger than that, you can most likely earn yourself some headroom by optimizing the server's setup.

Swapping from Apache to an alternative server type such as lighttpd or nginx is a good option for improving your dedicated server or VPS's performance. You should think carefully before changing your http server, and make the change only if you are familiar with the intricacies of running a server.

You can read more about the most popular alternatives to Apache here:

- ◆ Lighttpd: http://redmine.lighttpd.net
- ◆ Nginx: http://nginx.net

A good comparison of the two servers can be found at http://www.wikivs.com/wiki/Lighttpd_vs_nginx.

While both the servers mentioned above have smaller footprints than Apache and should offer better performance, there are some issues you should be aware of.

Firstly, Apache often comes preconfigured on most servers, and it has most of the configuration options you would need set out of the box. Lighttpd and Nginx require more configuration, and it can be difficult for inexperienced system administrators to troubleshoot certain issues with the server's configuration.

Secondly, Lighttpd and Nginx do not use the .htaccess file. This means you will need to convert the mod_rewrite rules used by WordPress MU and bbPress to the format used by your server. For example, the Lighttpd rewrite rules for WordPress MU look like the following:

```
server.error-handler-404 = "/index.php"
url.rewrite-once = (
    "^/(.*/)?files/$" => "/index.php",
    "^/(.*/)?files/(.*)" => "/wp-content/blogs.php?file=$2",
    "^(/wp-admin/.*)" => "$1",
```

```
"^/([_0-9a-zA-Z-]+/)?(wp-.*)" => "/$2",
"^/([_0-9a-zA-Z-]+/)?(.*\.php)$" => "/$2",
)
```

If your site is performing well, but you're nearing your bandwidth limit, check that your theme files are set up in such a way that images and CSS files are cached by the browser. Also, look at using gzip compression with Apache.

If you are interested in improving your web server's performance, you can find some good information at the following URLs:

◆ `http://www.serverwatch.com/tutorials/article.php/3436911`

◆ `http://httpd.apache.org/docs/2.0/misc/perf-tuning.html`

You can test your server's performance using JMeter available at `http://jakarta.apache.org/jmeter/`.

Pop quiz – speed up your site

1. Which of the following can help you troubleshoot slow loading pages?
   a) The YSlow plugin for Firebug.
   b) The 3DMark benchmarking tool.
   c) Your server logs.
   d) The EFT Fitting Tool.

2. Lighttpd is:
   a) A small technomage demon.
   b) A faster version of the HTTP protocol, which is not supported by all browsers.
   c) An Apache plugin which you can use to speed up your web site.
   d) An alternative web server that is lightweight, fast, and useful for high traffic sites.

   Answers: (1) a and d, (2) d

Summary

This chapter has touched on some ways to improve the performance of your WordPress MU and BuddyPress installation.

Specifically, we learned how to use caching to speed up the page loading times of our site and ensure that the site can cope with large amounts of traffic. We also talked about speeding up page load times and reducing bandwidth usage by streamlining our theme, hardcoding some things that were previously dynamically generated, and reducing the size of the images that make up our theme.

We touched on some server-side optimizations and talked about alternatives to Apache, which may be useful for bigger sites.

We learned how to troubleshoot slow loading times, how to determine where the bottleneck lies, and how to fix it.

We also discussed tweaking your server setup and testing your site's performance.

Now that we've learned about handling large amounts of traffic, we're ready to look at troubleshooting and maintaining your site.

12
Troubleshooting and Maintaining your Site

Once you have your blog network up and running, you will need to maintain it. This involves keeping the site's databases optimized and keeping the blog, forum, and social network software up to date with security patches. Usually, upgrades are a simple process; however, sometimes things can go wrong during the upgrade process, and sometimes errors can appear even during the day-to-day operation of your site.

In this chapter we will learn how to do the following:

- Safely upgrade your site
- Troubleshoot upgrade-related problems
- Protect your site from hackers
- Report bugs and issues to the developers of the script in question

So let's get started...

Why worry about upgrades

Once you have your site set up and working, it can be tempting to leave things as they are, although the reasoning "why fix it if it isn't broken" does not always apply to web applications. Just because you cannot see something obviously wrong with the way your site is working does not mean there is not a security hole that you cannot see, which could be exploited by an attacker.

In general, it is worth upgrading whenever a new stable version of a script is released. If the new version is mostly full of cosmetic changes and new features, you can wait a while before upgrading to ensure that any teething issues with the new version are ironed out. However, if the new release contains security patches, you should seriously consider applying it as soon as possible.

The best place to get updates on new releases is the WordPress MU web site (`http://mu.wordpress.org`) and the web sites of the plugins that you are using. For convenience, WordPress MU will inform you of the release of any new versions when you log in to the admin panel. If you check the plugins page of your admin panel, you will often see messages about out-of-date plugins in there as well.

If you aren't sure whether to apply an update, read the release notes. Usually there will be a `readme.txt` and a `changelog.txt` with any major release. If security updates are mentioned, it is worth applying the patch as soon as you are able to. The WordPress MU forums are also a good source of information. You can find those at `http://mu.wordpress.org/forums/`.

You can keep up to date with security issues by reading the Bugtraq mailing list, which can be found at `http://www.securityfocus.com/`. This web site contains an up to date list of vulnerabilities and exploits for the most popular scripts and web applications. Usually, security experts will inform the software vendor before submitting their findings to Bugtraq, giving the vendor time to release a patch. If a patch does not get released in a timely fashion, you may find that the notification on Bugtraq will give you the information you need to fix the bug yourself—either by making some minor changes to the code of the application or by disabling a certain plugin or feature until a patch is released—to prevent your site from being vulnerable to attack.

Performing a safe upgrade

WordPress MU will usually display a message in the admin panel informing you when an upgrade is available and offering you the chance to upgrade immediately. This feature is very convenient and can save you a lot of time when it works. However, it does not work well on all web server setups and, when it goes wrong, it can cause a lot of problems.

Before you perform any kind of upgrade, you should make a backup. If you already have a backup strategy in place, then you probably already have an up to date backup of your web site's files, as things such as plugins and theme files don't change all that often. Still, your database will need to be backed up.

Before you perform the upgrade, you should put your web site into maintenance mode (which you can do using the Maintenance Mode plugin available at `http://wordpress. org/extend/plugins/maintenance-mode/`) so that your users don't add any posts or comments while the upgrade is taking place. Once the site is in maintenance mode, you can back up the database—either by using a WordPress MU plugin, phpMyAdmin, the cPanel backup tool, or your favorite database management tool.

Performing a database backup via the command line

If you have SSH access to your server, then performing a database backup via the command line is probably the fastest and easiest way. The syntax for performing a backup using mysqldump is as follows:

```
Mysqldump –add-drop-table –h localhost –u username –p databasename | gzip
-c > backup_wpmu.sql.gzip
```

Performing a database backup via phpMyAdmin

Performing a backup via phpMyAdmin is a good alternative if you do not have shell access. Performing a database backup via phpMyAdmin is fast and convenient for smaller databases. However, it does not always work for very large databases, as the backup process may time out if it takes too long, depending on how your server is set up.

To perform a backup via phpMyAdmin, log in to the tool on your server, select the database you want to back up, and click **Export**.

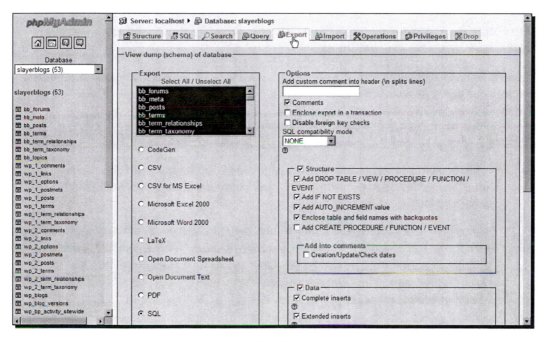

You can leave all of the settings at default, but it is a good idea to click the **ADD DROP TABLE...** option, and select some form of compression for the backup. Select **save as file** and choose a compression type. When you click **Go**, you should be presented with a box asking you where to save the file.

Store the backup somewhere safe. If anything goes wrong, you will need to import the backup later to get the site working again!

It's worth checking the integrity of any file backups you have, especially if you have made extensive changes to any of the files.

Time for action – performing the upgrade

1. Make sure that the site is in maintenance mode before you start this process. Ideally, you should have put the site into maintenance mode before taking a backup earlier in this chapter.

2. Go to your **Site Admin** panel. You should see a link at the top of the screen alerting you to the fact that there is a new version available. Click this link and enter your FTP details when they are requested. Once you've completed the upgrade, check your plugins page. If you see any plugins that are out of date, upgrade them using the **upgrade automatically** link.

[Screenshot of a WordPress Manage Plugins page in Windows Internet Explorer showing "The Slayer Cafe > Manage Plugins — WordPress". The page displays plugin management interface with the following visible content:]

Plugins extend and expand the functionality of WordPress. Once a plugin is installed, you may activate it or deactivate it here.

Currently Active Site Wide Plugins

Plugins that appear in the list below are activate for all blogs across this installation.

Plugin	Version	Description	Action
BuddyPress	1.0	BuddyPress will add social networking features to a new or existing WordPress MU installation.	Deactivate Site Wide
		There is a new version of BuddyPress available. View version 1.0.1 Details or upgrade automatically.	
What Would Seth Godin Do	1.7	Displays a custom welcome message to new visitors and another to return visitors.	Deactivate Site Wide
WP Auto Tagger	1.3.2	Automatically finds tags based on your post content.	Deactivate Site Wide
WPMU Enable bbPress Capabilities	0.1	Enables bbPress member capabilities when a user is created within WPMU. This allows immediate login as a 'member' after a user is created in WPMU.	Deactivate Site Wide
Plugin	Version	Description	Action

Plugins that are enabled site wide can only be disabled by a site administrator.

Currently Active Plugins

Bulk Actions ▼   Apply

Plugin	Version	Description	Action
Adsense Share for WPMU	1.2.3	Share Adsense income with your wpmu users. This plugin is based on work done by Mike Smullin. By Ishara.	Deactivate
		↑ Activate Adsense Share for WPMU Site Wide	
Advertising	3.4.7	Control and arrange your Advertising and Referral blocks on your Wordpress blog. With	Deactivate

http://localhost.localdomain/wp-admin/update.php?action=upgrade-plugin&plugin=buddypress%2Fbp-loader.php

Problems with the upgrade?

If the upgrade fails for any reason, check the developer's site (usually linked in the plugin's description) and download a copy of the plugin so that you can try installing it manually.

What just happened?

You have just upgraded your WordPress MU installation. In most cases, the upgrade goes smoothly. That being said, make sure you test all aspects of your site after you have finished updating everything. This is especially important if you are upgrading WordPress MU, BuddyPress, or bbPress. Sometimes the developers change or remove functions, which plugin developers may have relied upon in the past. Usually, developers are given a lot of warning about these changes, but sometimes they don't update their code before the new version comes out. So, you may find that some of your plugins behave unusually after an update.

Don't let fear of plugin problems put you off upgrading, especially if the new version includes security updates. Keeping your user's data safe should be your first priority.

Troubleshooting—when upgrades go wrong

If your upgrade does not work as you had hoped, then there are a few things that you can check. First, look at your `.htaccess` file. Sometimes, WordPress MU does not correctly update this when changes are made. Usually, an error in your `.htacces` file will either lead to a 404 Page Not Found error, or a 500 Internal Server Error. If you suspect that your `.htaccess` file is the source of your problems, take a backup of it, and then rename `htaccess.dist` to `.htaccess`. In the `.htaccess` file, you can see a line that says this:

```
RewriteBase BASE/
```

Edit the file so that the line simply reads like this:

```
RewriteBase /
```

The `htaccess.dist` file is distributed with the WordPress MU install and has all the default settings. If your `.htaccess` file is broken, then restoring this file will fix it. As our WordPress MU site has been installed to the root of our domain, we removed BASE so that the rewrite rules would point to the right URL.

Solving database connection issues

If you see an error like the one shown in the next screenshot, then this most likely means that there is a problem with your `wpmu-config.php` file.

If you get this error, the first thing you should check is the contents of your `wpmu-config.php` file. Make sure that the username and password provided are correct. Also, check that the server's hostname is correct. In most cases, it should say "localhost", but some web hosts such as GoDaddy do use remote MySQL servers. If those details are all correct, check that you can connect to the database using phpMyAdmin.

If you can't connect using phpMyAdmin, then it is likely that there is something wrong with MySQL on your server. If you're running a VPS, restart the MySQL. Depending on the OS of the server in question, we have two probable syntaxes. The first syntax is this:

```
service mysqld restart
```

The second possible syntax is as follows:

```
/etc/init.d/mysqld restart
```

If you aren't using a VPS or dedicated server, contact your web host to ask if they are aware of a problem on your server.

Diagnosing unusual error messages

If you see an error message instead of the blog, or in place of some of the content on the site, don't panic! Read the error message and take a look at the file that the error message belongs to.

For example, if the error message says:

Parse error: parse error in /var/www/slayers/wp-content/plugins/featured-posts.php on line 45

Load up that file, and scroll down to line 45. The chances are, the error will be right there or on one of the surrounding lines. Look for missing semicolons, unclosed brackets, and missing quotation marks.

Another error you may encounter involves "undefined functions". For example, see the following error:

Fatal error: Call to undefined function get_blog_posts() in /var/www/slayers/wp-content/plugins/featured-posts.php on line 27

This error means PHP doesn't know anything about a function called `get_blog_posts`. This is because the function in `wpmu-functions.php` is actually called `get_blog_post`. In this case, the error was created when I was making some changes to the plugin. I was tidying up the code and I turned the function name into a plural by mistake. However, you could see this error appear if a function gets renamed or merged into another function as WordPress MU evolves.

Error Message: Headers already sent...

One common error message that can be difficult to track down is "Headers already sent". This error message means that the server has sent headers to the browser before WordPress MU was finished preparing them—usually because of something simple such as some white space in the wrong place. If you have edited any files recently, make sure that there is no white space before the opening `<?php` tag or the closing `?>` tag. If you have just updated a plugin or updated WordPress MU itself, check the files that have been changed. Even a single space or line break in the wrong place can cause this error.

Troubleshooting—common problems

Sometimes problems can crop up that are seemingly unrelated to any changes you have made recently to your site. Tracking down problems of this kind can be difficult, unless you approach the issue in a systematic manner.

If you have not changed anything on the site yourself, the most likely causes of unusual behavior from your web site are file permissions and caching.

In this section, I will give some examples of issues that my clients have encountered with their web sites:

- **Users unable to add photographs to posts**:

   If your users are complaining that they are unable to add photographs to their posts (but the uploads seem to be completing successfully), then the first thing you should check is file permissions. On some servers, new files and folders are created with 644 permissions; ensure that the files are being uploaded to a folder with 755 permissions.

- **Slow loading admin panels**:

   After you have performed an upgrade, if you find that your site's admin panels are running slowly (especially the ones not connected to the main blog), then you should first try disabling any unnecessary plugins. Also, access each admin panel individually and confirm that the upgrade script was executed correctly on all of them.

- **I can't see any posts!**:

   If you can't see any posts, or searches return no results when they should have returned some, then you may have a problem with your browser's cache. Your cache might have stored a blank result. You can fix this problem by clearing your browser's cache and cookies.

◆ **Registration emails aren't going out**:

If your users aren't getting their registration emails or password reminders, then you should check the SMTP configuration of the mail server. If you don't have an SMTP server set up, install sendmail (or ask your host to do it for you).

Time for action – restoring a backup

If you decide to restore a backup, you can do this either via the command line or via phpMyAdmin. For very large backups, using the command line is a good idea; however, if you don't have command-line access, phpMyAdmin is a good option.

1. Go to your site's phpMyAdmin page.

2. Select the database on the lefthand side. For SlayerCafe, the database is called SlayerBlogs.

3. Go to the **Import** tab.

4. Select your database backup, and **click Go**.

What to do if your upload times out:

If the upload times out, you can use the **Partial import** feature and tell the importer to skip the lines that were executed during the first attempt.

What just happened?

You have just restored a database backup. Hopefully, you will never need to do this on your live web site! However, you may need to do this if an upgrade goes wrong or if your server crashes for some reason. If you ever need to move web hosts, perhaps because your site has become so popular that you have outgrown your original host, you could use this method to move the database to your new host.

You can also use phpMyAdmin to fix certain database problems (such as optimizing tables, as discussed in Chapter 11) and to make changes to the database if the site is offline.

For example, if you decided that you wanted to move your site to a different domain, you could set up the other domain, upload the database, and then use a simple SQL query to replace all instances of the old domain with the new one (for example, all instances of slayercafe.com with slayerbistro.com).

Protecting your site from hackers

When you put your site up on a server that is connected to the Internet, it instantly becomes a target for attackers. A popular web site is more likely to be the victim of a focused attack, but even a small web site is at risk from mass exploitation attempts where attackers scan every host they can find in the hopes of coming across something vulnerable.

Patch regularly and use good passwords

The best way to keep your site safe is to stay up to date with security updates and keep your server's settings as secure as possible. Limit the number of people you give admin access to and enforce secure password policies.

For example, don't use the same password for your blog account, FTP account, and the MySQL database for the blog network. Also, make sure each password contains a mix of letters and numbers (and a mix of upper and lowercase characters, if possible). The longer the password, the better.

Limit what your users can do

If you allow your users to upload files, limit the kinds of files they can upload to ones that are not likely to contain anything malicious.

If you are going to allow your users to customize their layouts, either limit this to simple CSS changes or moderate all theme changes by having someone look over the user's code submission before allowing it to go live. Allowing users to edit the theme files (or worse, the plugin files!) at will is very risky. There's nothing to stop the user from running malicious code on your server and possibly causing serious damage to your database.

Avoiding social engineering

Once you have locked down your server, the easiest avenue of attack is through your users and your staff. Social engineering is a favorite technique of hackers. Even technically brilliant hackers who know lots of ways to break in to computer systems sometimes try social engineering first. After all, why risk exposing a vulnerability that has so far gone unnoticed (thereby making the systems administrator patch it), when you can get into the system just by asking a poorly trained staff member for their password?

A common technique for social engineering attacks on web sites is to pose as a moderator or staff member. You may have seen phishing emails coming from `systems-administrator@ myemailprovider.com`. Hopefully you haven't handed over your passwords, but there are lots of computer novices who would believe that an email coming from an official sounding address is the real thing.

You can protect your users by preventing people from signing up with official sounding names. The option to do this is found under **Site Admin | Options** in the **Site Admin** panel.

On SlayerCafe, we have banned the following usernames: Watcher, slayer, vampireslayer, root, admin, administrator, register, blog, activate, support, techsupport, tech-support, members, watcherscouncil, email, council.

The list is not exhaustive and includes many usernames that sound authoritative only to vampire slayers. You should change this list for your site, adding in any names that may fool your customers (for example, an ISP may want to block names such as "billing" or "email-support").

If you are using a premium subscriptions feature on your blog network, then you should test it extensively to make sure that only those people who should have access to certain pages are able to view them. In the past, some member site add-ons have had a lot of holes or backdoors (although most of these have now been fixed). If you have a "printer friendly" plugin, make sure that users can't access premium content by using a "printer friendly" version of a link. Make sure that users whose memberships have expired really do lose access to pages that they should no longer be able to view; test your pages logged in, logged out, with JavaScript turned off, and so on. If everything behaves as you would expect, then you can be confident that your membership site stands up well to at least a cursory test. You should still keep an eye on your logs for brute force attempts and, if the software supports it, you should set up your member site script to lock out any user who fails to enter their password correctly a certain number of times in a row.

Pop quiz

1. Social engineering is:

    a) Building a web site for people to socialize.

    b) Promoting your site on social services such as Twitter, Digg, and Facebook.

    c) Hacking a web site by trying lots of different usernames and passwords until one works.

    d) Hacking a web site by posing as a technician, or otherwise tricking a user or staff member into giving out their details.

2. If you see something like a Fatal Error or a Parse Error you should:

    a) Panic! I'm not a programmer and I'll never solve this.

    b) Reinstall WordPress MU; it's the only solution.

    c) Read the error and look at the file it's referring to—the error is probably down to a missing bracket or semicolon.

    d) Retrace your steps and replace any files you recently edited with a backup. You do take backups, right?

    e) Panic! If the error was fatal, my server could be a vampire after sunset.

Answers: (1) d, (2) c and d

Getting help online

If you believe that you have encountered a bug in WordPress MU or in any of its plugins, then it is a good idea to report your findings to the developer so that they can fix the problem for you and any other users of the script or plugin.

For WordPress MU, you can find support at `http://mu.wordpress.org`. You can also read in-depth information about WordPress MU at `http://codex.wordpress.org`.

Most plugin developers will provide their contact details (either a web site address or an email address) in the plugin's `readme` file. So, if you have an issue with a specific plugin, check that file for details. Some developers maintain a presence on the WordPress MU, BuddyPress, and bbPress forums, while others prefer support requests and bug reports be sent via email or as a comment on their blogs. There are some premium plugins on `wpmudev.com` and, if you have an issue with those, you should use the support features offered on that web site.

Before you raise a bug report, it is a good idea to search the WordPress MU forums (or the forums at `buddypress.org` if it's a BuddyPress issue) to see if others have already encountered the same bug. Often, you will find that several other people have already posted about the issue and hopefully a workaround has been found.

If you cannot find any posts relevant to your problem, then you can make a post yourself.

Have a go hero – posting to request support

The people who offer support for open source web applications do so on a voluntary basis. They are not paid staff and are taking time out of their day to help you with your problems. The support forums get a huge number of posts each day, and it's easy for a post to get lost in the noise or ignored if it is too vague or difficult to read.

To maximize your chances of getting the help you need, you should be polite, offer as much information as you can, and indicate any measures you have already taken to try to solve the problem. You should also try to post in the most appropriate section of the forum.

For example, consider this request:

HELP!!!! BLOG WONT LOAD!

This request will probably be ignored or at least not treated with priority over more descriptive subject lines.

Consider the post subject:

500 Internal Server Error after Upgrade to WP-MU 2.8

This is much more descriptive and will likely get a faster response.

Inside the post, you could say something like the following:

I upgraded from WP-MU 2.7.1 to WP-MU 2.8, and I am now getting a 500 Internal Server Error when trying to visit user profiles. The front page loads fine, as do blog posts. It's only user profiles that have issues. My MU install uses subdomains.

I have checked my .htaccess file, and all seems fine. The contents are as follows:

> *<paste .htaccess file here>*

I searched about this issue and found others with similar problems who were running bbPress and BuddyPress. I followed the instructions for reinstalling those, but that didn't help. Any suggestions would be much appreciated.

Thanks.

A post such as the one above gives those who are in a position to help you the information they need, and it indicates that you have tried to solve the problem yourself but found that the posted solutions did not help you. This avoids people suggesting things that you have already tried.

When making such a post, it is a good idea to remove any information that is specific to your server. Pasting a `.htaccess` file is fine, but if you are asked to post the contents of your `config` file, you should replace the database username and password details with "MYUSERNAMEGOESHERE" and "MYPASSWORDGOESHERE" in the forum post, rather than giving your username and password details out to the thousands of readers of the forum.

Sometimes you will get a response to your query within a few minutes. Other times, it could take a day or so. It depends on how busy the forums are and how complicated your problem is. If you do not get a response to your post within a day or so, it can be tempting to "bump" it—that is, to make it appear at the top of the list of recent posts by posting a reply yourself. Before you do this, read the sticky posts in the forum to check the rules. In general, bumping too frequently is frowned upon.

If you are going to email a developer, it is doubly important to provide as much information as possible and to be polite. Developers of popular plugins will get a lot of email about it and, while they would love to be able to help everyone, they most likely have a job, family commitments, and hobbies taking up a lot of their time. If a developer doesn't answer you instantly, don't assume they are being rude. It's much more likely that they simply haven't had a chance to read their plugin-related email yet.

Summary

In this chapter we discussed some common error messages, and we also talked about how to upgrade your WordPress MU installation safely.

Specifically, we learned how to take backups and how to restore a backup if things go wrong. We learned about the auto-upgrade feature and how to put the site into maintenance mode while upgrades are taking place. We talked about some common error messages and what they mean, and we learned how to write an effective support request that will maximize the chances of your getting a speedy response, making it easier for the people giving you tech support to understand your query and offer useful advice.

We also discussed how to restore your site to working order if things go wrong.

Now that you have a working blog network and know how to keep it working well, you can focus on improving it, expanding it by offering new features to your members, and growing the community so that your members get as much as possible out of the site.

Index

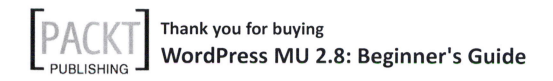

Thank you for buying
WordPress MU 2.8: Beginner's Guide

Packt Open Source Project Royalties

When we sell a book written on an Open Source project, we pay a royalty directly to that project. Therefore by purchasing WordPress MU 2.8: Beginner's Guide, Packt will have given some of the money received to the WordPress project.

In the long term, we see ourselves and you—customers and readers of our books—as part of the Open Source ecosystem, providing sustainable revenue for the projects we publish on. Our aim at Packt is to establish publishing royalties as an essential part of the service and support a business model that sustains Open Source.

If you're working with an Open Source project that you would like us to publish on, and subsequently pay royalties to, please get in touch with us.

Writing for Packt

We welcome all inquiries from people who are interested in authoring. Book proposals should be sent to author@packtpub.com. If your book idea is still at an early stage and you would like to discuss it first before writing a formal book proposal, contact us; one of our commissioning editors will get in touch with you.

We're not just looking for published authors; if you have strong technical skills but no writing experience, our experienced editors can help you develop a writing career, or simply get some additional reward for your expertise.

About Packt Publishing

Packt, pronounced 'packed', published its first book "Mastering phpMyAdmin for Effective MySQL Management" in April 2004 and subsequently continued to specialize in publishing highly focused books on specific technologies and solutions.

Our books and publications share the experiences of your fellow IT professionals in adapting and customizing today's systems, applications, and frameworks. Our solution-based books give you the knowledge and power to customize the software and technologies you're using to get the job done. Packt books are more specific and less general than the IT books you have seen in the past. Our unique business model allows us to bring you more focused information, giving you more of what you need to know, and less of what you don't.

Packt is a modern, yet unique publishing company, which focuses on producing quality, cutting-edge books for communities of developers, administrators, and newbies alike. For more information, please visit our website: www.PacktPub.com.

WordPress 2.7 Complete

ISBN: 978-1-847196-56-9   Paperback: 296 pages

Create your own complete blog or web site from scratch with WordPress

1. Everything you need to set up your own feature-rich WordPress blog or web site

2. Clear and practical explanations of all aspects of WordPress

3. In-depth coverage of installation, themes, syndication, and podcasting

4. Explore WordPress as a fully functioning content management system

5. Concise, clear, and easy to follow; rich with examples

WordPress Plugin Development: Beginner's Guide

ISBN: 978-1-847193-59-9   Paperback: 296 pages

Build powerful, interactive plug-ins for your blog and to share online

1. Everything you need to create and distribute your own plug-ins following WordPress coding standards

2. Walk through the development of six complete, feature-rich, real-world plug-ins that are being used by thousands of WP users

3. Written by Vladimir Prelovac, WordPress expert and developer of WordPress plug-ins such as Smart YouTube and Plugin Central

4. Part of Packt's Beginners Guide series: expect step-by-step instructions with an emphasis on experimentation and tweaking code

Please check **www.PacktPub.com** for information on our titles

WordPress 2.7 Cookbook

ISBN: 978-1-847197-38-2   Paperback: 316 pages

100 simple but incredibly useful recipes to take control of your WordPress blog layout, themes, widgets, plug-ins, security, and SEO

1. Take your WordPress blog to the next level with solutions to common WordPress problems that make your blog better, smarter, faster, and more secure

2. Enhance your SEO and make more money online by applying simple hacks

3. Fully tested and compatible with WordPress 2.7

4. Part of Packt's Cookbook series: Each recipe is a carefully organized sequence of instructions to complete the task as efficiently as possible

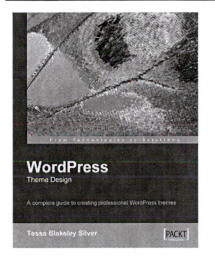

WordPress Theme Design

ISBN: 978-1-847193-09-4   Paperback: 224 pages

A complete guide to creating professional WordPress themes

1. Take control of the look and feel of your WordPress site

2. Simple, clear tutorial to creating Unique and Beautiful themes

3. Expert guidance with practical step-by-step instructions for theme design

4. Design tips, tricks, and troubleshooting ideas

Please check **www.PacktPub.com** for information on our titles

Breinigsville, PA USA
05 December 2009
228651BV00003B/5/P

9 781847 196545